of WITCHES

of WITCHES

CELEBRATING THE GODDESS
AS A SOLITARY PAGAN

JANET THOMPSON

SAMUEL WEISER, INC.

York Beach, Maine

First published in 1993 by
Samuel Weiser, Inc.
Box 612
York Beach, Maine 03910

99 98 97 96 95 94 93
11 10 9 8 7 6 5 4 3 2

Library of Congress Cataloging-in-Publication Data

Thompson, Janet.
    Of witches : celebrating the Goddess as a solitary pagan / by Janet
Thompson.
            p.   cm.
    Includes bibliographical references.
    1. Witchcraft.   2. Goddess religion.   3. Paganism.   I. Title.
    BF1566.T456   1993
    299--dc20   92-45542
                                                            CIP
ISBN 0-87728-762-7
CCP

Cover painting is *Astarte Syriaca* by Dante Gabriel Rosetti from the Glasgow
Art Gallery and Museum. Used by kind permission of the Bridgeman Art
Library, London.

Printed in the United States of America

This book is for my daughter Kelly,
who loves as the Goddess intended.

Table of Contents

Acknowledgments

I wish to thank Dr. Amore for his critique of the origional thesis. His open-minded approach to the work encouraged me to continue.

Many thanks to those friends whose support and good wishes made me realize that I could do it. Special love to Gary, Krystal, Dina, Ian, Judy, Andrea, Connie, Veronique, Jamie, Greg, and Paddy.

Thanks to those witches who have written about the Craft for the benefit of all.

And special love to Marian and Scheff who taught me to question.

May the love of the Goddess be with them all.

—J.S.T.

The Promise of Tomorrow

A halo of silver 'rounds a brilliant Moon,
while the dry leaves blow.
The Moon is pale and full of power,
an essence beyond comprehension,
an incredible force of magic.
Times like these
leave the very center,
that shelters the spirit,
the temple of center, the temple of energy.
On and on we travel to find the fork
in the paths that divide.
One direction and you will find fate—
having passed aside lessons richly taught.
The other road—fate will find you,
and in turn you will discover your destiny.

Your rewards will be great
and the path, your salvation.
Experience your destiny and the windows will open.
Stretch out your arms and embrace the reality
of knowing,
for the only reality is learning.
Hold it close to your heart,
and draw the energy—
to seek more.
Look upon the horizon and
recognize the promise of tomorrow.

Introduction

I chose to write this book for two very different reasons. This work (the thirty original pages) started out as a thesis. I enjoyed writing and the only aspect that I found tedious was searching out sources for all of the things I had written from memory. It reminded me of the idea of asking a Christian to source and footnote the Lord's Prayer. And so, to once again state the Wiccan intent of goodness and to remind the reader that there is a religion of Wicca was my first intent. The second reason is simple. When someone has interests or beliefs that are out of the "norm," then one seeks out as many viewpoints on the subject as one can. This is true of most Wiccans I have ever met. Most are voracious readers who gobble up as much information as they can. This way a working base is established and the learned witch is then equipped to write his or her own rituals, spells, and celebrations. But there must be a grounding of knowledge from which to work. And for a solitary witch or coven who has not had the opportunity to meet other witches, books are a must.

I wish to bring Craftsmen and Craftswomen closer together so that we may share with and enlighten each other. Only through the passing of knowledge can we hope to achieve the unity that is required to fix this planet. Too much is negative in the world. We must see life as an interaction with the Mother. Pagans, whatever tradition they follow, are the ones to show by example. We have our essence in the Earth and Moon. We thrill with the dawn of each new season. Our souls are irrevocably linked with the Mother. And what's more, we are aware of this.

We must work together as never before. We must learn as much as we can, and continue to do the good works that need to be done. If we can pass love and joy from the inner place that is inside every pagan, we can enrich other lives as ours have been.

The experience of witchcraft as a healing and gentle religion, is very clear to those who practice it. There are, in all religions, rituals or traditions that perhaps only practitioners see the value of clearly. The power raised in a Witch's Circle can be felt by those who are consciously receptive to it. The release of that power to the healing purposes for which it is meant can be seen by witches and non-witches alike. It spirals from sight leaving its aura for us to witness. These are the experiences of Wicca. As a Wiccan, I have witnessed many such releases and have participated in rituals too numerous to count, as well as actively researching the Craft for many years.

Each person must choose his or her own path to the Light. Some choose very organized and well-documented religious paths, while others find joy and peace in the lesser-known faiths that may be misunderstood. Wicca provides a legitimate and positive path for those who feel drawn to it.

> Eight words the Wiccan Rede fulfill,
> and it harm none, do what ye will.

Maiden, Mother, and Crone

The Lady has three and she shows them to you,
Youthful Maiden, Mother and Crone.
Remember Her in all that you do,
And you never will be alone.

The Maiden is huntress at the time of Beltane,
fires burn on hilltops ablaze,
She chases the King Stag, a babe to obtain,
a child for the Goddess, the Mother to raise.

The Mother, she waits for her children to grow,
teaching each to care for the Earth,
She brings them the knowledge that they all must know,
'till She is the Crone and awaits Her rebirth.

The Crone she is aged and bent o'er her cane,
wisdom is her duty to leave,
She must impart all that she's obtained,
The Lady awaits her and Peace she'll receive.

[To be sung to the tune
of "Scarborough Fair"]

Chapter One

COMING TO WICCA

The way by which Wiccans come to the Craft and the incredibly varied opinions of authors in the field sparked this chapter. There are those who feel that you must be one of two types of initiate. If you have been initiated by an Alexandrian or Gardinerian witch, then you are welcomed. If you claim hereditary lines from your family line, then it is assumed you are a true witch. The very idea of someone being in the Craft by other roads is abhorrent to many Wiccan authors.

Many witches, however, have reached the path by other means and can be very powerful, indeed. All who stay on the Wiccan Way must be assumed sincere, otherwise they would have chosen a more fulfilling one. Being an active and practicing witch takes time and effort. There really is no such thing as a Sunday witch. You must work to increase your potential powers and you must take time to learn. Wicca is a life system as well as a practical religion. It must be used to be strong.

Some witches have memory of another lifetime lived as a witch and feel that the Craft is still within them. They may not have a mother or grandmother to show them practical work, but with the help of books and friends of the Craft, they develop their own style and interpretation

of this poetic and healing life. These people I call Reincarnational Wiccans.

Others feel their roots through family lines or feel
ancestral geography strong within their blood. Their
ancestors may have had a brief or lengthy interlude within
the arms of an organized faith, but the line is one
descended from pagan roots. Mind you, as Margot Adler
has pointed out, if we go back far enough, everyone's
ancestors were pagans. But in this case I am talking on a
more immediate basis. These witches I refer to as Ancestral Wiccans. Their sincerity and devotion to the Craft is
not within anyone's right to question or judge. Other
witches should use their powers of tolerance and understand that ancestral Witches are just as Wiccan as they
are.

There are others still who really cannot identify the
source of their inspiration, but choose the path because it
provides them with personal growth and peace. There are
many fine self-initiation rituals available today and they
express the Craft clearly in their symbolism. These witches
cannot be judged by others either, because every witch
knows that it is the sincerity and honesty with which you
do your work that is the key factor. If self-initiated witches'
work is filled with non-destructive forces, and they keep
to the Rede, then, indeed, they are witches.

There are many, like myself, who have a pull to the
Craft from a combination of these ways. I am an Ancestral
Witch by birthline, and my relationship with the origins of
my family are deep within me. On the maternal side, I
claim Craft through solid Celtic lineage. My people were
not aristocrats and were probably land folk. The land folk
were and still are very Craft-oriented. The festivals are still
celebrated — or, at the very least, recognized — alongside
the Christian holy days. On my father's side, I come from

a long history of land folk in Hungary. These people became very Christian, but were still very much involved with the seasonal changes and pagan traditions.

I recognize myself as a Reincarnational Witch through a long series of regression sessions and spontaneous memory. My work is peppered with sudden remembrances of methods from long ago. I find myself reaching for specific herbs that I have not used before, but with which I have had previous intimate bonding.

My degree from university is in the classical tradition and in philosophy. My draw to things Greek, Roman, and Egyptian has been a lifelong passion. The education I received was like coming home, and many of my regressions revealed lives in these periods. I was not Cleopatra, nor a princess, nor anyone famous; on the contrary, I was involved in the religions of the ancient world, in a place that set me far apart from the general populous.

I am a High Priestess of Third Degree in Celtic tradition. My teacher and initiator achieved Crafthood from a Priestess of Celtic hereditary lines. The main problem with the idea of a witch of any contemporary line is that one cannot be 100 percent sure of the unbroken continuation of each through Europe and into Canada and the USA. We must trust our instincts and judgment when it comes to working with someone. We cannot ask for a personal history from everyone we meet. How a person reaches the light is irrelevant in the long run. Just as a Christian finds peace through faith, witches find peace through Wicca. If the Rede stands firm in the mind of the witch—and it harm none, do what ye will—then the witch is true.

The measure of a good witch is not the method of a spell, nor is it the way the person reached the Craft, *but lies in the effort and sincerity of the practitioner*. I *know* that I am a witch. None need believe me but neither do they have the right to judge me. My work and human relationships prove that I would die before deliberately harming anyone or anything. I do powerful spells when they are needed. I find joy and peace in my work and from the Craft in all respects. That is the bottom line. I cannot stand to see Brothers and Sisters of the Craft quibble about who is more Wiccan than whom. It does not matter so long as we all work toward our peaceful goals together. I find in my interludes with other witches that many find peace and are happy to converse in the Craft. Others are so busy espousing their credentials that they seem to forget the main purposes of the Craft, and that is the healing and humane work we are avowed to carry on.

Many authors have contributed books on the Craft in simplicity so that those who wish to follow the path may do so without the fear of needing elaborate surroundings or written knowledge of some obscure language. Some write about the Old Country practices and the lovely seasonal festivals that have been held for thousands of years. Others write books with elaborate ritual that greatly enhances the atmosphere of the Circle for many. Whatever the contribution may be, each witch has a talent and if the intent is clear and pure, then the work that we can accomplish as a community of colleagues and friends in the Craft is limitless. We have the power to literally change the world. We can educate, give talks, and encourage care of the Mother. We can continue to advocate environmentally sound practices and attitudes. We can contribute to our communities in the tradition of the Old Ways. We can provide spiritual encouragement and care. We can spread love and healing no matter what the scale. By enhancing our own lives with the peace of Wicca, we enhance the lives of those around us.

We can pass on a respect for the Mother. We can show our children, by example, what is required to ensure a green planet in the future.

People come to my home for readings, classes, workshops, or just to visit. Many have made the comment that they leave feeling as though they have been recharged; they feel rejuvenated. This is not something I deliberately try to achieve, but rather, through my work I emit a great deal of energy that they must absorb when they spend time here. I have also been told that on occasion I glow! This is the light of the Goddess reflected in my eyes. I feel her within me. I feel safe in the lessons she is conveying to me. The path to the light does indeed come through one's eyes no matter what that path may be. If it is built on love and integrity, then it will shine through, lighting the hearts of those it touches.

That is not to say that we never have upsetting or negative periods. On the contrary, we are human and react in human ways. But because of our strong faith, we may deal with the negative in more immediate ways than others do. Our work is immediate but the effects may take time. Despite this time, we know we have done the work and can therefore relax with the knowledge that it will be taken care of.

The microcosmic work of one witch is a part of the healing done by all. I wish that all who practice a sincere form of the Craft would look upon others as a family for that is what we are. Families can be separated by miles and lifestyles, but they are still connected. So are witches. Like it or not. We are children of the Goddess and therefore are under Her tutelage. We can live in harmony in the Craft and we must strive to do so.

Doreen Valiente, in her book *Witchcraft for Tomorrow* says: "You have a right to be a pagan if you want to be."[1] The Universal Declaration of Human Rights (Article No. 18) states that everyone has the right to freedom of "thought, conscience and religion."[2] Ms. Valiente has made a great contribution to the religion of Wicca. And she is right. The freedom to worship as a pagan is anyone's, and we each should be tolerant of another's choice.

If we are drawn to the concept of the Old Religion, then we should learn all we can and explore all avenues of research. A coven is not necessary for a practicing witch; there are many powerful and learned solo witches who practice alone either by choice or because of isolation from possible covens due to geography. Wicca provides for all the voids of religious confusion if there is an attraction to the Craft. The Circles and rituals and Sabbat celebrations provide for the physical and psychic senses. The spells and divination encourage the mind to grow.

The side-effect to starting on any new path, is of course, the written works which may or may not be available. Once the interest is piqued, the path is clear. Witchcraft provides growth and that is the key in any pursuit; to grow within yourself and to know your own potential. And like any learning pursuit, you can plod along for a time without really feeling a part of it. Then one instant flashes and you realize that you have been a part of it all along, and it is this instant that enhances your entire existence. It may take incredible patience, and seem like a great deal of work. But one day something washes over you and the understanding flows. This is what happens with religion. For some, the feeling hits the first time they

---

[1]Doreen Valiente, *Witchcraft for Tomorrow* (Custer, WA: Phoenix, 1978), p. 22.
[2]*The Universal Declaration of Human Rights* is a document published by the United Nations, setting forth a universally agreed upon list of Human Rights.

expose themselves to a religious philosophy or event. Others may take years to feel as though they finally have answers.

The Charge of the Goddess has many beautiful passages. But perhaps, the most important passage of all is: "For I am the soul of nature, who gives life to the universe. And thou who thinkest to seek for me, know thy seeking and yearning shall avail thee not unless thou knowest the mystery; that if that which thou seekest thou findest not within thee, thou wilt never find it without thee."[3]

The witch knows that she or he must find the answers within and so enters the Circle with an open heart and an open psyche in order to communicate with all of the aspects of the Self and to direct those aspects in their manifest forms.

The eight words of the Wiccan Rede are the *only* dogma of the Craft. If the witch, in daily life, can continually follow this law then he or she is, indeed, a powerful witch. These words however, must be kept in mind not only in one's actions toward other people, but must be part of one's thoughts as well. All negative or evil—be it thought or deed—will come back threefold and must be worked out at a future time. Witches do not want to deal with return negativity, so few generate it. As with all balancing systems, if a human is inclined to good or virtuous behavior, then this, too, will return to the sender.

Contemporary witches, in these times of hurry and pressure, find themselves in tune with the Morrigan or Great Earth Mother. This entwinement with nature and the natural cycles of the seasons, Sun, and Moon, gives witches a sense of harmony. It puts us in tune with our

---

[3]Janet Farrar and Stewart Farrar, *A Witches Bible*, Volume 1 (New York: Magickal Childe, 1981), p. 43. If you don't have this book, the current version is called *The Witches Bible Compleat*.

own body as a microcosm and allows us to experience that microcosm in relationship with the macrocosm.

It is this relationship that concerns witches the most. The knowledge of what lies behind the mundane world allows us to know what we must do to enhance our physical existence and to ensure that our mistakes are not repeated. This is the essence of the Craft; to be in touch with our fellow humans, to get in touch with the lunar and solar cycles, and to return to harmony with Gaia. The Witches Wheel (Sabbats) are completely structured around the changing of the seasons and the solar leaps. There are eight yearly Sabbats—four Greater Sabbats and four Lesser Sabbats. The summer solstice, winter solstice, vernal equinox, and autumnal equinox make up the Lesser Sabbats. The Greater Sabbats are *Imolg* (Candlemas), February 2nd, *Beltane*, April 30th, *Lughnasadh*, July 31st, and *Samhain*, October 31st.

The twenty-eight day lunar month provides the witch with a cycle in which to practice the arts. The Sabbats are festivals for sharing and celebrating, while the lunar *Esbats* are a time for healing work and psychic development.

As the moon has three faces, so does the Goddess. The Maiden aspect of the Great Lady corresponds to the waxing of the moon, the Mother aspect to the ripe beauty of the full moon, and the Crone aspect to the waning moon. The Goddess rules over all. It is from Her in the Morrigan that we come and to her we return. The God is, as well, represented in more than one manner. The god of the Sun is the power of the seasons without which we could not exist. He is also represented as the Horned God of the forest and of the hunt, stemming from a time when humans were reliant on the earth and Her creatures as well as the seed, root, and bud. Representations of the Horned God existed millennia before the Christian Devil.

Therefore, the Pan of paganism cannot be the Satan of the Christian belief.

There is another factor involved here. To worship or build a religion around Satan, one must believe in Satan. This, witches do not do! Bad deeds stem from the system of karmic checks and balances and not from the powers of an evil creature or mock deity. Those who practice Satanism or "celebrate" an inverted mass or Black Mass are considered by witches to be very wayward individuals. The very crux of our faith tells us that we cannot harm another person nor can greed take over our use of the elemental power for which we strive. It is simple—we would be writing our own misfortune. Wicca is a loving life in its own right and we do not need to parody another.

Because of the tie that witches feel to Earth, one would not find many witches, male or female, who are not outspoken activists for ecology. Our concerns are great. Gaia will not withstand the punishments that the human race has imposed on her. She is breaking down and if we don't do something right now it may be too late, ". . . and physicist Max Bjorn's painful assessment will have been proven true: that Nature's attempt to evolve a thinking Creature on this earth has failed."[4]

As a parent, I have a grave responsibility to my child to try to ensure that she has a clean and stable environment even after I am gone. This is a responsibility that I take most seriously. Just as our children are learning that it is not "cool" to smoke, so must we teach them that the Great Mother is not to be enslaved to humankind's purposes. We must learn to live in harmony with Her for She is our provider, and if we destroy Her, we destroy our-

---

[4]Susan Weed, *Healing Wise* (Woodstock, NY: Ash Tree, 1989), p. viii.

selves. There are many who feel that this is the reason for the great return to the pagan religions. To get in touch with Gaia and ourselves is one way to reverse the damage that has been done.

The striving toward a greater solo or collective psyche is the basis for the witch's work. In addition, to disperse the power raised by the psyche is the purpose of ritual. The at-one-ment of ourselves with our universe is a way to achieve the power we need to do the work required. And this work cannot be achieved as readily in an unbalanced world.

Stewart Farrar, in *What Witches Do* concludes his book with his feelings of the Craft. ". . . I find its symbolism beautiful, its ritual satisfying, its tolerance (and indeed encouragement) of individual attitudes civilized . . . and its successes impressive. For me it offers a practicable synthesis of the needs of the individual; the interests of his fellow man, and the meaning of the universe."[5]

---

[5]Stewart Farrar, *What Witches Do* (Custer, WA: Phoenix, 1983; and London: Sphere Books, 1971), p. 190.

Chapter Two

THE WITCH AT WORK

A witch's magic circle is a deliberately created space, which—once in place through ritual—becomes a "part of all worlds—attached to none." It is sacred to witches who use it as a magnetic energy containment field.

There are two very unique things about being within the magic circle itself. The first is that everything matters within its circumference. The second thing is that the atmosphere that fills it completely should be one of perfect love and perfect trust. Everyone must provide a piece of the harmonic puzzle that is the circle. The greater the atmosphere of the circle, the more powerful and intense the work becomes. Yet, between the working times in circle, there is a great deal of love and laughter. Pure water or wine is sipped as everyone relaxes and rejuvenates themselves.

It takes personal energy to build a circle and to maintain the power there. This is hard work—be it done by a solo witch or a coven. You must build it by pouring all you can from your own store of energy and everything you do in the psyche will, of course, manifest itself in the physical. Therefore, fatigue and thirst are understandable physical side effects to the expenditure of power. Every ritual should be seen to in as great detail as is possible, but the standard rule of thumb is that the greater the work required, the more prep time and personal wellness is required from the witch.

In every circle I have cast, I always have complaints of the room being too hot at the end of the rituals. I explain to every complainer that the area outside the circle is normal room temperature. Invariably they have to experience this effect for themselves and it is enjoyable every time to watch them. The portal is opened for them to step through and the look that crosses their faces is worth a thousand words. Not only have they worked hard, but now they are presented with a clear example of the physics involved in the metaphysical world.

When the power is released to its purpose and the circle banished, all those within it generally feel a marked difference in the temperature.

Another unique feature about being in the circle is that there is little or no concept of time, and the witches within have no awareness of the passage of time. The magic circle stands (or rather floats) as a microcosm of this world and the next, and occupies a place between them. It must be visualized as a ball or sphere rather than a circle having a two-dimensional geometric shape. This sphere acts as a portal to many dimensions and magical places. It yields incredible knowledge when used properly. Here the witch can work while maintaining a direct link to the etheric and psychic planes.

This direct link causes the man-made concept of time to "stay" outside the circle that is cast. When we participate in a circle we often have no idea how much time has elapsed. This can have a disconcerting effect, rather like mini jet lag. A bath, using the water element, is a great way to regroup. The water takes care of your physical weight (buoyancy), and the mind can pull itself back to the mundane world. This is an example of using the elements and elementals to center and focus.[1]

Witches believe that the world beyond what we see, feel, and live in, is filled with the elements and creatures that will do as requested. These are not evil creatures nor would any witch try to call up something evil. They are the archetypical representations of the forces within every person, and are able to manifest in a way that enables the invocator to communicate with them. Through this communication, we are able to use their energy and element representations in our work.

Many witches argue that the elementals (not elements) are creatures of ceremonial magicians. But most witches that I have talked with tend to agree that by taking a visual representation long used in occult traditions, the element, its uses and power, becomes much stronger. Visualizing animate beings enhances our work. Elementals are powerful beings in their own realms, and when they are called across the threshold, they are at the direction of the witch who summons them.

Their usual manifestations in the psyche are seen throughout history. Trolls represent the element earth, and they dwell in earthy places, such as caverns and below the roots of trees. They are dwellers of the shadows and the damp misty places where the earth swells and shades trolls from heat. They are creatures that keep to themselves. They gain their power through a constant connection with Mother Earth.

Salamanders represent the element fire. Their movement reflects the nature of their being; they are quick and

---

[1]Elements are the realms of earth, air, fire, and water. Elementals are the visual or psychic representations of these realms.

elusive as fire, itself. They move as a flame, darting here and there with sureness of movement. They draw their power from fire and disperse it with no waste.

Sylphs represent the air element. The realm of air is the most vast and it is vacant at first glance. But when in Circle, the realm of air is filled with creatures that at first are just shadows and mists. The power of air is as the wind. It can be helpful or hurtful, but a witch will use the air element for positive purposes.

Mermaids or water nymphs represent the element water. Water is a flowing motion of individual units. The water of the psychic realm is—by its nature—a soothing element. It is one of cleansing and purity.

Each of these realms is directed by the point of a compass. The earth elements lie in the north of the Circle, the fire in the south, the water in the west and the air in the east. Each realm has an overseer who is generally referred to as the Lord of the Watchtower. The Lords of the Watchtowers are the guardians of the Witch's Circle. They have a twofold purpose—the first being the guardian aspect, and the second relates to the power raised. The Circle is divided into four regions, and each Lord contributes to the power raised within that region. They reach out into the planes beyond the Circle and pull into it the power that the witch needs.

The elements are put to ritual use every day by everyone. When we bathe or shower, we step into the warm water with a preconceived idea as to how it will feel. We want to relax and enjoy the feeling of the water and therefore this preconception brings about the actual event of the experience of bathing. We have literally created a spell to ensure the benefits of the bath. We do the same with the other elements many times in our daily life. The witch just isolates these times so they can have the greatest benefits.

The idea of the power of the elements and of elemental creatures scares some people. Many people feel that these invoked creatures can turn against the caller. However, I must reiterate that these things come from inside us, therefore, they are as good or evil as we ourselves are. No self-respecting witch that I know is of the nature that would enable the elements to turn. The things that a witch uses are in sync with the nature of that witch. The intentions of the witch are the indication of what nature the invoked creature will display.

The symbolic representation of witchcraft is the five-pointed star with a single point topward. The inverted pentagram (or two points topward) is the common contemporary symbol for satanic worship. It is the inverted pentagram left at the scene of so many heinous crimes today, used by people who need to leave a symbol of mind sickness, of evil deeds. Witches are not responsible for these actions as they are not the work of a Craft community.

The pentagram of Wicca is a representation of mind over matter and of the power that human beings must learn to control. The uppermost point (that of spirit) is shown as having dominion over the four elements of the mundane world.

The Witch's Tools

The working tools that a witch uses within the Circle are (or should be) extensions of the arm. As I have mentioned before, none of the tools about to be discussed are completely essential. Every witch at some time or other has probably built a Circle without any tools. This happens when one is in danger, or when one is just out for a twilight stroll. I will discuss each piece with the idea of a fully dressed Circle, so that you will understand how to work properly with the tools available to you.

As most of you will already know, it was important for the witch tools to look as part of a "household" during the "burning times." All tools had to be disguised as objects of everyday use in the home. To have any designated ritual items meant death to the practitioner. This is probably beyond our comprehension as we do not experience the intense persecution our ancestors did. We take for granted our freedom to worship, vote, and we voice our minds the way we can. Today we can have our witch tools exclusively for the magical purposes they are intended, generally without fear.

The tools are consecrated and are used only for their specific purpose. If they are used properly, they will become a part of the Witch's being. Each of the four major tools corresponds to an element and to a suit in the tarot deck.

The *athame* is a representation of the element fire. In the Tarot it is the suit of swords. The *pentacle*, which represents the earth element, corresponds to the tarot coins. The *chalice*, is, of course, the water element, and represents the Tarot suit of cups. Finally, the *wand*, holds the realm of air, and the suit of rods in the tarot.

Many contemporary witches find that the wand is one of the last tools they obtain, partly because a Circle can be created and banished without it, and partly because a witch will wait for a wand to make itself known. By that I mean that most wands come to a witch and not the other way round. I found my wand while out walking by the river beside my home. It happened to be exactly the right length and would not have felt better had it been custom-made.

Once obtained however, the wand becomes limitless in its uses. I use my wand to draw to me anything that is invoked, to increase my awareness when scrying by passing it over the objects I am reading from, and to cast, or build a circle. I use it to draw power to a particular plant that may be ailing, or to wave over my daughter while she is sleeping to insure protection the next day. The tarot, the Witch Stones, a piece of jewelry or a cauldron of water are all methods I enjoy using for a reading, and my wand only serves to enhance the effectiveness of the tools I have used.

The wand is also used for casting non-protective circles. By this I mean a circle strictly used for love or peace or celebration when protection is unnecessary. A fine example would be the circles used for a wiccaning or handfasting. Neither of these occasions requires the protection that the athame affords. Protection for the bride and groom in a handfasting come from cutting the wedding cake with the athame, which is the only time it is used to cut anything.

The tools that a witch obtains should be picked out by that witch and the athame and pentacle can be presented at the initiation. If these are available for a self-initiation, then one way to maintain the idea of presentation is to wrap them in black cloth (to maintain their mystery) about a week in advance, and then at the appropriate time in the rite, the tools can be unwrapped, consecrated, and used for the first time. Seeing them in Circle with the glow of the candles shining in them can be a moving experience and can instill in the psyche of the new witch how important they will become to the work that will be done.

Wherever you obtain your tools, make sure that they feel comfortable to you when you hold them in your hands. If they feel at all uncomfortable, then perhaps you can try again in a few days time. If they still feel wrong, then you are best to try elsewhere. Trust the vibrations you feel in them. You will know when they feel right. You will know what is best for you.

One favorite place to pick up magical tools is in secondhand shops. Every city has them and some are better than others, but keep checking back because this is one type of shop where the stock constantly changes. Look carefully, for most of these stores are greatly overcrowded and you could overlook a great find. One wiccan friend of mine has found some marvelous things at junk shops and garage sales. He once had the luck to find a great hammered copper cauldron. The bowl part sat on the backs of three rams. The dish was large and open which made it perfect for scrying. It could be held in the hands and felt very comfortable. It was an excellent find and we used it for many rituals.

This same friend also found a beautiful gong which we used in place of a bell for many of our seasonal rituals. Its tone is deep and delightful. Once you have cleaned and consecrated your things, they can greatly enhance your work.

I will discuss the tools one at a time to give you a detailed description of the tool itself, its use, its significance and the beliefs connected to it. But please keep in mind as you read, that the tools of the witch are, in essence, the things that the Mother provides. They are the things of earth, air, fire, and water. They are the phases of the Moon and the seasons of the Wheel. Tools and trimmings are nice to have but not necessary. Most witches regulate the use of different tools by checking their emotions and the events to be done in Circle. They will equip their altar according to how they feel and what is being done. Never in a Circle have I observed "dead baggage." The decorations and tools used are needed. Each thing comes into play for the kind of ritual or work involved.

The Athame

The athame is the first tool to be discussed, mainly because traditionally witches receive their athame at initiation, if they have one. It is the one tool I would not want to do without. The athame that I have has a solid copper handle, which gives it a nice weight for working. Most traditions call for black handled knives, but a witch may use whatever is comfortable for him or her. Many witches have goat-footed athames, ivory handled, or metal handled. As with all else, it depends on the witch who is using it.

The first thing a witch should do with the athame is to take it to someone to have the blade dulled. This is a grave necessity as working in Circle with four or more witches can be dangerous if every blade is sharp.[2] The athame is designed as a tool that does no cutting whatsoever. It is only used for this purpose, as stated earlier, for the ritual cutting of the handfasting cake. This ensures protection for the witch pair as they head out into the world conjoined.

The athame is the representation of the fire element and has the function of "power sent." By this I mean that it is used in such a way as to maintain and send power, cast Circles and protect the witch during ritual. The wand, on

---

[2] I saw an accident happen when there were only three of us in the Circle and the cut was nasty. It is best for both the solo and the coven if the blades are dulled and then everyone can be sure of safety.

the other hand, is a tool of reception of power. It draws power on a basis of love, whereas the athame draws power on the basis of its strength to be sent to do work. It sits as the tool of the south quarter of the Circle for those who do not have a sword. In general, the athame and the sword are interchangeable for most work. It protects the witch and is used anytime that psychic force is used, such as in the ritual of degrees. An initiate is asked to symbolically face the might of the athame or the sword to show his or her loyalty to the Craft. Please note here that I did not say loyalty to the coven or group, (loyalty to the coven should be automatic before even considering initiation). Loyalty to Craft means that the new witch will keep safe the things that fellow witches share and will strive to learn all that he or she can before trying anything without support or supervision.

In the case of a self-initiated witch, the part of the ritual I refer to—using the sword or athame—can be performed solo. The athame is held up with the point poised at the heart and the symbolic pledge is made. The witch must learn to keep his or her own council when it comes to work which, if talked about, could damage or harm someone.

The athame is also the representative of the male force of the All. In the symbolic Great Rite, the athame is lowered into the cup (the symbolic female force) to enact a spiritual or cosmic intercourse. It is in this ritual that the laws of polarity are recognized to their fullest in the Circle.

One confusing aspect of the symbolic Great Rite is that, during the ritual, the priestess holds the athame and the priest holds the cup. This is done to stress the representations of the positive and negative polarities on the etheric planes. The entire reasoning behind this ritual is the emphasis of the equality between the sexes and all opposites in the Craft. It can be a very moving moment in any ceremony.

If you are "shopping" for an athame, please remember one thing. Take some time with the tool you feel drawn to. Ensure that the draw is not just aesthetic but spiritual. The athame is the extension of the witch's arm and must feel totally right. Hold it in your hand, close your eyes and try to pick up its vibrations. It will serve you well if the two energies can merge and are compatible. When you get it home, if you are already a witch, then clean it, polish it, dull the blade, consecrate it and enjoy. If you are a solo self-initiate, then you must clean it and dull the blade, wrap it in black cloth and wait for your initiation ritual. If you are a novice awaiting an initiation, then you must clean and dull the blade, and put it away. Your High Priestess will instruct you on what to do with it when the time comes.

The Wand

The wand corresponds to the element of air. In the east quarter of the Circle, we find the realm of air, and the wand is a "lightening rod" for that realm. It draws the power and maintains it for the witch to use. It absorbs its represented element and sends it to your work as you command. It is usually made of wood although there are some beautiful metal wands that have been made and decorated by the witch who will use them. The wand is one of the more liberal of the tools. It can be anything which feels right. The wooden ones are generally inscribed with witch symbols and drawings. I found the easiest way to inscribe my wooden wand was to heat a piece of metal in a fire or by my stove and to burn into the wood the symbols that I wanted.

Many wands are the length of your arm from the middle finger to the elbow, but this is not mandatory. I have one branch that I love, which is very long and looks something like a medieval walking stick. A staff is effective for visual impact at a ritual, especially one that is designed to invoke love and strength, healing with zeal.

The wand is thought to be the longest used tool by the human race. This would be a very logical conclusion considering the mother races of paleolithic humans. What they had was tree branches, stones, animal bones, etc. A magical wand would naturally come about because it would extend the mogul's arm for the rituals they practiced.

The wand, during the "burning times" was concealed as the staff of a broom standing in the corner of the cottage. The broom is a traditional witch item. Everyone, of course, had a broom for the standard household required one. In the witch's cottage and many a farmhouse, the broom was a tool used for seasonal celebrations and magical operations. It was used, not to fly to the Sabbats, but to ride through the fields to show the crops how high to grow. This was strictly an agricultural exercise to ensure the prosperity and supplies for the village.

The broom has also been used for sweeping the area of the Circle for some ritual and for handfastings. This ritual sweeping is to symbolize the sweeping out of all negative influences for the event or couple.

The broom is used in small magical tasks, too. If you want a guest to leave, provided it will not harm them, then place your broom at the door and they will leave, usually within a half hour. If you wish to receive a message that you have been waiting for, then put the broom in the north corner of your ritual area, and the message will come within one cycle of the Moon. There are many little samples of such magic and they are limited only by your imagination. Each will provide you with what you are looking for, on the condition that the motive is pure.

The Pentacle

The Pentacle is a disk-shaped circle of copper, or wax, or wood. In the old days it was drawn in a bowl of earth or formed from wax, as both could be easily destroyed if in danger. Today, a pentacle can be purchased in most occult shops or new age book stores. It has a pentagram engraved in its center, surrounded by the other major symbols of the Craft—such as the symbols for the Goddess and Horned God, the kiss and the scourge, and others. Some pentacles are highly polished while others look well worn. My pentacle is the one tool that I never polish because the only thing that is generally in contact with it is salt. Salt is a dry ingredient that holds much power, therefore it leaves residual on the pentagram. I find that my pentagram is strengthened by this residue and I have no wish to cleanse it.

Because it is the representation of the earth element, the pentagram corresponds to the north quarter of the Circle. This is the area where the altar is usually placed and the pentagram sits in the center of the altar. The north quarter is the entrance for the Goddess, as well. It is from the altar quarter that she emerges and is evoked into the High Priestess.

When charging or consecrating a particular item, place it on your pentacle on the altar. This is an old tradition and imbibes the object with incredible power. There are a few rituals in which I carry the pentacle around the circle for presentation to the Watchtowers but these were designed and written by me.

The Cup or Chalice

The cup is the representation of the water element and corresponds to the west direction. Its only relationship to the Christian chalice is its development through the myth of the Holy Grail. In her book, *The Mists of Avalon*, Marion Zimmer Bradley portrays the myth of the Grail beautifully.[3] She obviously did incredible research and is in agreement with many of the historians, anthropologists, and researchers who feel that the Court of Arthur, with its deep pagan roots, knew the Grail to be the Chalice of Immortality or the Cup of Cerridwen. Cerridwen, with her masculine counterpart, Cernunnos, were the Goddess and God of early Celtic paganism. Hers was the cup of everlasting life.

The cauldron is interchangeable with the cup in that it is a representation of the rebirth of human beings. It is the female tool in magic and is used for the burning of a small fire at many of the festivals. The cauldron can be any pot with which you feel comfortable. Be sure that it will safely hold fire and use it with care. I have a small black cauldron on three legs which I use for my own work in the Circle and when more than one is working I use a lovely pot that was given to me by a witch that I know. It is heavy pottery and withstands the small flames which I build in it.

The cauldron is also used for scrying, and when filled with water, it can yield a great many triggers for your psyche. I will often darken the water with washable black

---

[3]Marion Zimmer Bradley, *The Mists of Avalon* (New York: Ballantine Books, 1985).

ink to give it greater depth and thus provide a better "screen" on which to see things. When scrying, I find it helpful to place a chosen crystal from my collection at the bottom of the cauldron. This serves to draw power into the pot so that the emanations from it are greater. You can choose any stone which would correspond to the questions you are trying to answer.

The Cords

The witch's cords are his or her spelling companions. Cord magic is probably the most often used kind of work done by witches or covens. I have a collection of seven different colors that I use all the time. There is a white, red, green, blue, violet, orange, and brown cord on my altar. I prefer the thick satin cord to any other as it is workable and attractive. The color importance should be known by Wiccan readers, but will also be discussed in the chapter on spells and rituals.

Often a group of witches will do cord work by joining their cords in a center knot with the ends stretched tightly. The cords are then held by the witches in a wheel and the power is pushed to the center, while intense meditation and visualization is practiced. The High Priestess will give a loud command when she sees that the power has built to a crescendo and the witches will release it to its goal. This method is called the Witches Wheel.

Cord work to the solo witch is a bit different. The cord can be used as a Ladder. This is a series of knots on the cord and each day the witch touches each knot and repeats the spell. It is an incredibly reinforcing program. Cords can also be used to wrap around a packet of the items for the spell to charge them with a spiral casing.

Candles and Incense

Candles and incense are, of course, both enjoyable and functional. A candle generally sits at each of the quarters of the Circle and two sit on the altar, with the north directional candle in the middle. Candles are the fire element within the Witch's Circle. They do not work in the same capacity as the sword—which is the tool representing fire. Candles are actual fire *providers*. Often, a witch will use two or three candles in the cauldron in place of the fire called for. They light the Circle with a magical glow and most everyone is susceptible to their charm. They enhance the power being built, and they make scrying a more focused art by placing a candle behind the scry tool. Most witches I know usually have a candle going in the home or covenstead all the time. I will often have the two altar candles lit while I am home. I am very careful about fire safety while I am out of the house, but the seven day novena candles with the inserts are perfect for leaving on if your work requires a candle lit for a specified time. My mother has been quite ill over the past five years at different times and I like to keep a candle there for her. She knows its message and takes solace from it.

Incense is a representation of the air element and the incense is usually taken around the Circle to cleanse and purify the area. Hanging incense burners on chains are not expensive but do marvelously. The incense emitted from a variety of herbs being burned is the vehicle which will carry the requested work to the Goddess. I will often combine different herbs—chosen for their magical properties—and burn them in the cauldron while chanting an incantation for the desired results. Herbs are very powerful for scent magic and have been used for as long as people have existed. The medicinal properties of the herbs are well known and if you are interested in herbalism, research thoroughly. If possible, try to find someone who is knowledgeable and willing to show you the herbs. First hand is the best way to learn. Don't depend on photos in a book. Try a few teas to start. Ointments are relatively easy and get good results. But please be willing to learn without forging ahead on your own. Medicinal herbalism is an art unto itself, so go with care!

Incense is chosen according to the magical properties desired, or according to personal taste. But if you take the time to mix a special blend yourself, then its potency becomes stronger. The scents that are available today are unlimited in their variety. Choose one or two and see if you like them. This way, you can build up a library of scents and their properties and you will have gotten to know them.

About Dress

There are many debates within the Craft as to whether a witch should be skyclad (naked) or clothed. Those who use the skyclad method feel that robes distort and detract from the psychic power raised. They add that the idea of everyone being the same contributes to the democratic attitude of the Circle. Many witches feel, however, that to make and use robes appropriate to the ritual being performed adds to the deep concentration of power. I prefer working robed and have a few favorites. Some witches like working robed when in Circle with others, and skyclad when alone. So it all depends on your own comfort and tastes. Whatever will enable you to enhance the connection to the Old Ones is acceptable, provided, of course, that it harm none.

Most witches I know enjoy wearing a necklace both in the Circle and out. I have many different ones that I use depending on the occasion. Often I will just wear my pentagram. Men and women alike will wear pentagrams, Egyptian symbols, and some handmade pieces. (Although in this part of the world, the art of smithing is not often practiced and prices at a designer jeweler's can become outrageous.) Many witches use shell necklaces for different water rituals and these can often be made from your own gatherings.

One of my favorite working garbs is a long black gown which is sleeveless (I find the energy generated in Circle provides more than enough heat), and with it I sometimes wear a small cape of material (the color suitable to the work being done) attached to the shoulder straps. I wear my cord (red or white most often) around my waist and the appropriate necklace, bracelet, and earrings. I find this attire the most comfortable, and it enhances the work I do. Clothes, or lack of them, are not the issue here. How you appear in your Circle is merely a means to an end. There are no rules regarding attire in the Circle. The force that is built is strictly dependent on the sincerity of the witch and the amount of concentration brought to bear. A thin layer of cloth is not capable of stopping the energy or power I emit, so the robes cannot impede my work.

Everything that is used as a magical tool or accessory is there to enhance the strength of your work. They all give powerful cues in magic. Make use of these cues and they will serve you well.

A Covenstead

The covenstead is essentially any place that the coven or solo witch practices the Craft. If this is the living room of your house, then your home would be the covenstead. Where the coven convenes is entirely up to its members. It may be that you are lucky enough to have a permanent outdoor spot. If that is the case, then the home of the high Priestess is likely to be referred to as the covenstead. The ritual tools and coven material would be kept here and therefore any indoor rituals would probably be performed here as well.

The word *covenstead* is essentially a trigger to bring about certain feelings among coven members. Feelings within each witch and about each witch are what the covenstead is all about. It is the attitude of the witch to the working place—one of goodness and light. Whether a Circle is at that moment cast, the atmosphere prevails. Therefore the witch carries the love and joy throughout the home. There are subtle similarities between witches' homes which will be discussed later, but essentially the message here is that wherever the covenstead may be located, it is a place where power is built and dispersed on a continual basis and should be treated as a place of respect.

When a coven or solo witch is moving into or leaving a covenstead, it is important that a cleansing and opening ritual should be done at the site of a new area, and a thorough cleansing should be done when leaving a work area permanently. You would not be kind if you left behind so intense a vibrational area. The new tenants must be allowed to fill the space with their own energy and thus it is your responsibility to clean up after yourself.

This is considered polite in the same way you would clean the refrigerator before moving out.

We must leave the area cleansed for one other reason. The energy you form in a covenstead is powerful, and as such, acts as a link to its members. This link can become a danger for you if you leave it connected. Any tension in your old home, even if it's caused by the new tenants, could reflect back on you. They may not have a very happy home, for whatever reason. Therefore it is wise to disengage yourself completely for your own safety and peace of mind.

On Covens

The life of the solitary witch is what he or she makes it. It can be rich and fulfilling, with the road ahead viewed as the personal and enlightening experience which it is. Albeit, human beings can get lonely and in need of others with whom to communicate about shared beliefs. Loneliness can occur in a room full of people; we have all felt alone despite the number of people around.

Coven work can be very rewarding. That is not to say that the coven is the only road. Solitaries, who are such by choice, are working in a way most comfortable to them. Some people feel that their worship and ritual privacy is of the utmost importance. Others feel most fulfilled and powerful when working in combination with a group of other witches. They develop a common goal when healing or working, and feel comfortable in the presence of close friends. Although, as a Wiccan who maintains a covenstead including ritual work with others, I prefer, at times, to work alone. My bond to the outer and inner worlds is very strong when I can face myself on a level where the physical and material forces are virtually non-existent. I have to gaze into my own essence without the distractions that accompany the mundane. This exercise in awareness helps me confront inner turmoil and thus strengthens my motives for the work about to be undertaken.

The strongest structure a coven can begin with is a group of like-minded friends, whose feelings about each other are already warm and comfortable. These would be friends who can relate to the insecurities of others in the group. Human insecurity has a definite place in this setting. Others are there to help, comfort, talk, and listen. When we try so hard to mask our insecurities around people we do not know, we expend energy that could best be put to use elsewhere (such as healing, etc.). Problems are solved by friends working together with group effort. I have also known of covens that started by bringing together a group of semi-strangers. They have planned and written rituals, practicing as a group in the Sabbats and Esbats. However, these groups seldom stay together for the long haul.

If a novice or solitary is seeking to enter into coven-oath with others and has not had any experience with this, it is best to magically summon the opportunity to meet with one who will be a kind of guide. Each time we graduate to the next level of knowledge, we meet someone who can suggest reading material, introduce us to others, and be there to answer questions. Of course, I do not suggest that you close your eyes and ears to any opportunities, as these could very well be the results of your work.

When you are on a particular path, the needed teachers, mentors, and companions are sent when you are the most relaxed and confident in your own love. When intentions harmonize and the time is right, you will find that contact you have been seeking. This is repeatedly told by other Wiccans who came to the Craft from childhood religions. The people they needed to speak to just "popped up" and were there for them; so it will happen for you.

A strong thread that weaves itself through the life of the witch is the ability to have faith. Faith is that which generates the power and endurance of a spell; it is that which lends might to the weakened will. It is that upon which our entire existence depends. Human beings must have something to believe in or we die. Atheists believe that this is what is and there is nothing beyond. Catholics believe in the abilities of the Saints. Muslims have faith in the fact that Allah is creator and empowerment. We Wiccans must have faith and believe in what we do. Without the ability to believe in something, we are left with a less than positive outlook, thus creating (by ourselves) the atmosphere in which to breed dismay. And as negative begets negative, the trap becomes much harder to disarm. When we believe, we open ourselves to an entirely new horizon of possibilities. We keep our eyes open and we are assured through our faith that the right moment will present itself.

When considering coven-oath with others, carefully digest the sense of order and ethics involved with that group. There are many fraudulent and unethical groups around and only some are truly blessed with the right intent. Here are a few characteristics you will want to avoid.

• Be wary of the recruiters! Wiccans generally do not recruit their fellows. Wiccans do find each other, and therefore do not need to look for new members.

• If a group or leader of a group asks for money or valuables of any kind, question seriously his or her motive. Do not sign over any titles, deeds, securities, or bonds to any group or individual. Many so-called satanists who use the anti-christian stage as a cover for criminal activities, often demand personal properties and the above-mentioned documents of their membership. If you are unsure at all — do not join. If this group is legitimate and right for you, you will be presented with another opportunity.

• If a group demands that you appear skyclad (naked), bound, or blindfolded before ever meeting other members, or until you are completely comfortable — refuse! Force is not the manner of practicing Wiccans. We are a gentle people who would not convince another to exhibit uncomfortable behavior. The issue of skyclad or not is completely up to the individual. If you do not want to participate in nude rituals, you should not be forced to do so.

• Never readily volunteer your home for meetings with new people. You may open a crowded can of worms. Your home is your secure spot in the physical world. Do nothing to jeopardize this security. Get to know these people first.

• Look for traces of practicing black workings within the group's rituals. Just be aware of the symbols of satanic tradition and keep an eye out. The inverted crucifix, real blood used in ritual, the use of heavy drugs, bondage used against the will, the Living Altar, the use of snakes, mind bending hypnosis, or any other activity that does not sit comfortably with you should be avoided.

Wiccaning,
Handfasting, and Requiem

Wiccanings, Handfastings, and Requiems are the rites of passage which mark our lives. The blessing of a child, a marriage, and funeral rites are common to all and witches are no exception. Following is a brief description of each rite and its wiccan tradition.

Wiccaning

A Wiccaning can be a very joyous occasion. This ceremony is a blessing bestowed upon a child born to witch parents. The baby (or small child) is brought to the Circle (decorated for the event), and the High Couple blesses the child in the name of the Goddess and God. The Wiccaning is for protection, but it is also to ensure that the child will be properly educated in many traditions or religions. When he or she is of age, the child can decide what path works best. He or she is to make up his or her own mind, for any Path to the Light cannot be pushed on anyone. Each must seek his or her own, for we are not all suited to the same way of life. All gods are one god, and all goddesses are one goddess. It really does not make a difference which path is chosen, provided it fills you with light and joy. If you are angered or hurt, then it is not the right one for you.

In this ceremony, the child is appointed symbolic god-parents, and it is the duty of the god-parents to maintain a relatively constant protection for the child as he or she grows. I am not talking about a ritual every night, but a magical source of energy and joy can be sent out from the god-parents' home and recharged regularly. This tradition is a caring and loving one. Wiccaning serves as a blessing for the child.

Handfasting

Handfasting is a Witch wedding. This is a ritual where a couple is joined for a chosen time or a lifetime. Many High Priestesses are licensed to perform a wedding recognized by the county. A handfasting is a loving event. The couple is joined in a ceremony and there are many different ones. Some witches follow what has been set out in books and others write their own ceremony. There are a few traditions that are common to most rituals. The couple is symbolically bound together at the wrist to represent the bonds they feel; the symbolic Great Rite is generally performed, and the wedded couple is usually made to jump the broom. This is a way of ensuring that the couple start married life with all negative influence behind them. They jump into a life of love and joy.

Another tradition that is followed by most is that the covenstead sword or the High Priestess' athame is used to cut the wedding cake. This tradition is still practiced many places because brides in many cultures pick out a special knife that will be used at the wedding. Most bridal boutiques have this type of knife in stock. Some pagan traditions survive without being recognized as such.

The celebration following the handfasting is up to those involved. The traditional cakes and wine would be available and a toast to the Old Ones performed. The wedding cake would on these occasions be substituted for the standard crescent cakes. Dancing and laughter is also an essential element for every witch wedding.

The Requiem

The requiem for a witch or friends of a witch is strictly up to the person designing it. A requiem does not have to be given immediately after death. It can be performed up to one full cycle of the Moon following the passing of a loved one.

Losing a loved one is a universally heartbreaking experience. The feeling of loss and the sadness is almost unbearable. It is best to take a little time to adjust to the loss and to compose oneself before holding this service. Funerals and memorials are hard enough on the bereaved without trying do these things in a few days.

Most of us stand by our beliefs when we grieve. Our beliefs give us comfort and allow us the feeling that our loved one is peaceful and happy in the world beyond. The witch will say goodbye to a friend and allow the tears to flow. This applies to both sexes, as male witches are comfortable with their own tears. Witches perform a ritual enabling them to see that the loved one has reached the Land of Summer and rests in the arms of the Goddess, awaiting the next incarnation. The loved one is safe and cared for. The witch will bid farewell to the friend or loved one, knowing that the bond between them is stronger than death. The two will meet again and be rejoined.

The requiem is actually a celebration of the cyclical motion of the universe. The cycle of human life, from infant to elderly, is a continual process. We must be a part of it for our education. This is what a requiem is essentially about. Witches wear white to acknowledge the freedom and love that awaits the person who has died. Expect tears for people will cry, but in their hearts witches know that the loved one will never be far away.

Chapter Three

OF RITUAL AND SPELL

Ritual is the movement of a witch's belief. Chanting, drumming, lighting candles, burning incense, and casting circles are all rituals. Ritual allows us to pass to another time and follow the movement of Goddess-Blood in us. We hear the music in the background and we fly on the sound waves to another time and another place. We feel what those-who-have-gone-before experienced. The physical world around us disappears and we are hurtled through time and space to magical realms—to times when the mysteries were revered as a path of knowledge and wisdom. What steeps within the witch is the very pulse of the Goddess herself. Beneath us and around us is the Great Mother as she was then—alive with growth, clean and powerful. She vibrates with life. The priests and priestesses of all the pagan faiths could stir the blood of the children of the Goddess with a dancing prayer. They rejoiced in the bond between the Mother and themselves. They saw the changing seasons and celebrated them with ritual. They paid attention to the world around them. The leaf that turned red, the ground that became cold and unyielding—all these signs were observed and honored as a part of life.

The need to express an emotional reaction in a physical way is an inherent trait in all human beings. We must express ourselves in some manner—some cry, some laugh, some bite their nails or hide their reactions. All are ways of expressing what emotions lie deep within us. Ritual through dance, movement, chant, or recitation are also ways to help witches deal with everyday things that happen in our lives. It may take some time for new witches to open to the use of the Craft in everyday life, but with a deep faith in all that we try to do, and a continual awareness of our behavior and speech, the Craft will come into us one day and fill our souls. We realize with sudden insight, that we have assimilated the precepts of Wicca and we know that we are not aware of exactly when the transformation took place. We just know that deep inside and in all that we do, we accent everything with witchcraft.

Many things can be added to a home to create within it the atmosphere of harmony and joy. Through scent and candles, pictures that are pleasing, and areas that are comfortable and not busy, one can achieve a place where there is freedom to go within. That is where it all happens. We must seek our answers from within ourselves, for if we seek them from without, we will find nothing. The Goddess does not give us the answers, but facilitates our awareness. She allows us signs and clues that we must use to work the answers through to their deeper meanings. Through ritual we can disassociate ourselves from the world that surrounds us and fills all our senses with the 20th century. We can be in another time and place—a place that allows us to see inside and to rejoice in the learning. It gives us what we need to reconcile within ourselves those things that we have done which have a price. We can be conscious in a subconscious way. The alpha state allows our mind, our very person, to step outside this noisy, hurried world. A small act or ritual can provide a great deal of peace for the person from who's heart the ritual extends.

In Wicca, the ritual and symbolism is only as important as the practitioner finds necessary. Some Wiccans find gardening more fulfilling than ritual, while others would rather dance or chant as a way to touch the Great Mother. Each must find his or her own way of achieving the balance and harmony within the religion. Ritual, symbolism, and myth are each a way of bringing the deepest psychic and psychological visions to the surface.

For instance, if you have a very real desire to quit smoking and use Janet Farrar's method of spelling with chess pieces, you could create a visual representation of yourself and the cigarettes that are doing the damage. The chess piece would represent you and you would, with ritual, pour yourself into it. You would perhaps carry it with you for a time before the actual ritual, to strengthen the tie. You would then concentrate on the cigarette and see, feel, and present it as a dastardly enemy. The two pieces would then be put up on a shelf. With only about an inch between them, the quit-smoker would be able to see that they are together yet apart. Just as you and cigarettes are together yet are not good to each other. You would see, with each passing day, that the two repel each other, and are moved a little further apart. Each time you move the two pieces a bit further, you reinforce the picture of the goal you have set and this becomes a powerful motivating force. If you are certain of the power you hold as a witch and have complete faith in your own abilities, the spell will work.[1]

Of course, the psychological world recognizes the power of an individual's own psyche and uses many simi-

---

[1]Janet Farrar and Stewart Farrar, *A Witches Bible*, Volume 2 (New York: Magickal Childe, 1981), pp. 237, 238.

lar techniques for therapy. The quit-smoking packages that are advertised are numerous. Many of them work for many people. Each will be appropriate for a different type of person. When people have an intense desire to quit, then the thing they must be most conscious about is the method that will make this task as quick and painless as possible. To enjoy the companionlike relationship with a procedure that witchcraft affords, enables quitters to rely on something in addition to themselves when the struggle gets tough.

The witch uses what he or she knows and is most comfortable with (and let us not forget that anything done in Circle is powerful). So combining the Circle with the intensity of any spelling presents the practitioner with a massive base on which to firmly stand.

Spells

Within the Circle the witch will celebrate, make merry, communicate with the Ancient Ones, cast spells, heal, and do scrying and divination. The celebrations come at Sabbat times, but joy is a part of every Circle, or it should be. It is a time—after magical working—for good friends to share cakes and laughter. The communication with friends after a Circle is over is an extension of the peace we find in the circle. For the solo witch, the peace which follows a good celebration or working Circle is motivation aplenty.

The casting of spells is a great part of the witch's work. If, for example, the witch is healing, this can be done mentally, but the addition of props and symbology serves to enhance the power in the mind of the healer. Witches tend to believe that the words of a spell (especially a healing spell) can lose their effectiveness with the telling. Each time they are told at an inappropriate moment, their power weakens. This is why witches are counseled to be cautious. The four responsibilities attached to any magical act are—to know, to dare, to will and to keep silent. There are few variations to these in most paths dealing with magic.

The imagination is given a great deal of freedom when it comes to the writing of new spells and rituals. Generally the spell is written in rhyme because a chanting rhyme is not only beautiful, but it is very beneficial to the concentration of a witch. We repeat it many times as we build the power required. The more of oneself that is put into the spell, the greater its effectiveness.

The closest a witch would get to a "negative" type of working would be what is known as a binding spell. The spell would enable the witch to keep a particularly nasty person away. It would not interfere with that person's daily life, nor would it do the person harm. Think of it as a cosmic restraining order. It has the power to keep the person out of contact with the witch, thus the witch's environment is kept free of that person's influence. The key to all spellwork is checking and rechecking that no harm will come to anyone and the same holds true of a binding spell. Harming none is a grave responsibility to the witch. Every negative thought and deed returns to its sender. Therefore, to ensure a peaceful future, the witch must be positive in the present. Responsible witches have no wish to bring about their own misfortune.

Spellcasting is probably the most "mysterious" activity that witches engage in. At least to the general public, it is. This is one subject that I am questioned about most often. It is also one subject that my non-Wiccan friends tend to tease me about. There are some folks who do not see it as a "real" activity, just as many do not believe in the existence of spirits.

Spells do exist and they do work. It is as simple as that. There are literally thousands and thousands of witches worldwide who know this. I have a library full of books by different Wiccan authors that are full of spells that have been tried and have worked. Some are elaborate, others are simple country spells which are enjoyable to use because of their simplicity. Some have been written by the authors of the books and others have been passed down by family or tradition. Whatever way a spell comes to be, its effectiveness is totally reliant on the person performing it. I have included spells in this chapter that I designed and I can assure you, they work! They worked for me and if you use them with the right intentions, they will work for you, too. You can modify them for your own work, as you need. They are not gospel, but are presented here as a suggested method. Each has been used and has held to the task. But a word of caution—if you reword or revise them, be aware of the finished piece and make sure it harms no one. Never misuse any spell. Spells have a nasty way of rebounding on the witch who uses them if the spells are not sent with absolute love and healing.

I often find myself inventing new spells at the oddest times or in the oddest places. Every witch I have talked to has experienced this phenomenon. One spell I created was for a non-Wiccan friend who suffered from psychic vampirism. I devised a way to stay linked with her on a continual basis to alleviate some of the stress for a time. I put a charged crystal (citrone) in a bed of protective scent herbs. She used the protective mixture in her pot-pourri burner and placed the crystal in a spot near her bed. I was able to visualize the stone and instantly set up a reinforcing link. The incantations that I used for the spelling of the stone and the herbs were specifically designed for her so I will not include them here. However, if you keep in mind the goal of the spell and write your own words, try this method of protection and I am sure you will find it helpful. I have used this method many times, and I have come to call it the Crystal Connection, not only for the use of any particular crystal, but the word *crystal* means something important to my friend.

The methods of creating new spellwork is unlimited. I have used a leaf, cactus needles, pens, coins, keys, jewelry, and even a cassette tape. You not only have the incredible variety of plants and herbs available, but any object that suits the purpose. The thing to keep in mind is what you are trying to achieve with your spells.

Visual spells are those that require the use of a photograph, wax image, or poppet (similar to a puppet or doll). These things are not used for the purpose of hurting anyone. They are not meant to inflict harm on the recipient or to do any damage whatever. The image of a demented sorceror jabbing pins into image dolls isn't realistic!

Images are used to enhance the visualization of the person in healing spells, prosperity spells, and many other spells. The photograph is often used when group work is involved. It helps the group focus their thoughts on the person more intently. If it is healing that is being done, witches are better able to see the healing forces moving directly through the person by way of the photo. Wax images are made when the person or photo isn't available. They are also used in magic that requires a distinct period of time. Their one perfect attribute is that they can be disposed of after the work is done. For spells involving the transfer of negative forces from the client to the doll, they are great. With the negative or vampiric forces trapped in the doll, the image can then be magically separated from the client and destroyed.

Poppets are little dollies made of tightly woven material stuffed with a mixture of herbs appropriate to the work involved. They are cut in the general shape of a human and are made in the appropriate color. (See the Color Guide on page 54.) The witch devises an appropriate incantation and list of herbs to be used.

If, for example, the spell is for healing, then perhaps the list would include pine, nutmeg, marjoram, and coriander, all herbs of healing and health. These are broken up (do not grind them in the mortar, as they would sift through the material of the poppet) and stuffed into the dolly. The dolly is then placed on the altar for charging and the spell is worked. The poppet goes to the person the spell was worked for and that person keeps it until the work is done. If it is an ongoing health spell, the poppet should be returned to the altar every three phases of the Moon for recharging.

Visual or image spells are not dangerous if done with love, and are definitely not the working of black magic. They are a medium that can be used to enhance and strengthen a spell so that its effects are felt more quickly. They need not scare anyone, because a spell of any kind should never be done without the permission of the recipient.

There are cases where you must make an exception to this basic rule. Healing spells are often done with the patient *in abstensia*. Often the patient is not in a position to be consulted. But so long as the Wiccan Rede is strictly adhered to, then the love from a healing spell can only serve to help the person. There is no harm in trying and a person who is ill can use all the love available.

Cord work is a favorite of many witches. It is effective and provides the witch with a number of reinforcements. The color of the cord is important, as is the number of the knots you use. If I am doing a cord spell by myself, I enjoy using the cord spell devised by Doreen Valiente.

By the knot of one
    the spell's begun.
By the knot of two
    it cometh true.
By the knot of three
    thus shall it be.
By the knot of four
    'tis strengthened more.
By the knot of five
    so may it thrive.
By the knot of six
    the spell we fix.
By the knot of seven
    the stars of heaven.
By the knot of eight
    the hand of fate.
By the knot of nine
    the thing is mine.[2]

There are, of course, great powers in numbers and nine is the number of the All. It is the number of the Goddess, as is the number three, for Her triple aspects. There are many good books available about the power of numbers, and a witch, with research, will find what works best for the type of spell.

---

[2]Doreen Valiente, *Witchcraft for Tomorrow* (Custer, WA: Phoenix, 1978), p. 188.

Cord work done in a coven or group situation is potent and visibly strong. Anyone who has developed the ability to see auras can witness the build-up of power in a Wheel if it is done properly. The participants keep their mind tuned into the goal and the leader or High Priestess keeps her eye on the power that is built. At the appropriate moment, she shouts a command and all the witches push the power to the center. From there it is released to do its work. The Wheel is wonderful in a group because it not only takes a fairly small space to perform, but everyone is involved in the same way. The group dynamic is enhanced and each person is responsible for equal amounts of power. It is also pleasing to feel the energy flow from one person to the next in a smooth circular motion—a circle without beginning or end. Continuity is a wonderful by-product of the Wheel.

When I tie up little packets of herbs to be used for a spell—or as a talisman—I use a cord spell with them. I will tie an appropriate number of knots in the cord that binds the packet with a one line incantation to strengthen the herbs inside. The easiest way to make these is to cut squares of material 7″ × 7″. Black is often used because it is the absorbent color—a universal recipient. Place the herbs you are using, along with a token representation of the spell's goal, in the center of this square of material. For instance, if the packet is being made for a prosperity spell, the token you may want to use would be a coin. Coins are a representation of money and prosperity, as well as the metal of the coin acting in conjunction with the herbs to strengthen the spell. Metal is forged from the earth and the element of earth is strong, indeed.

When you are finished with the filling, gather the corners of the cloth and bind the pouch with the cord, using the number of knots you decided on before starting. The packet should then be carried by the person for whom the spell was cast. When the packet is no longer needed, it can be burned in the cauldron, or the contents can be tossed into running water (minus the coin, of course).

In many cases the cloth can be used again. If the spell is for financial help, the packet material can be used for a similar spell again. This, however, is when the packet was only used by you. This ensures that it will not be used for alternative purposes. To cleanse the cloth, immerse it in a pan of boiling water and add a dash of fennel seeds. Leave it for a few minutes and pass your hands over it when it is done. Hang it up and dry it and it will be ready for use again. Many witches argue that spell materials should not be recycled, but I feel that the Goddess will grant our spell even though we may recycle some things. She must be sorely disappointed in the treatment of the planet and I will do everything I can to alleviate the problem. My power is easily strong enough to completely cleanse a piece of cloth, a coin, or a sheet of recycled paper. Most witches I have met are strong enough also. I know that She understands why I do this.

These little herb packets are wonderful for protection of the home. They are hung over doors, beds (you can obtain herbs to aid in sleeping, as well!), and in closets or drawers.

Here is a recipe for a protection packet filling that has worked wonderfully in the past. The herbs used are found in most kitchens so there will be no expense. The herbs can be substituted with others of similar property, if need be. I would, again, suggest a token such as a small pebble or crystal. A pebble is a smaller version of a rock or field-stone, and they were once used to build and fortify castles and keeps. Pebbles, therefore, represent that kind of protection.

Recipe for Protection Packet

One part dill
One part corn kernels
One piece of cinnamon
One/half part basil
One part rosemary

Hyssop and agrimony (one part each) can be incorporated if you have them. Make your packets and as you hang them about your home, spell them with your incantation. The herbs should, of course, have been charged between your hands prior to their use and the packet material will have been consecrated. For added protection, leave them on your altar for a few days. Every full cycle of the Moon, take each one and break up the contents to release the scents within. This will help recharge the packet.

Element Spelling

Element spell work is among my favorite kinds. This method requires a small amount of salt, water, ash from incense previously burned, and a used match. It is quick and easy to do and does not have to be done in any particular way.

Take these things to your sacred spot or altar and charge them on your pentacle. Let them rest there overnight if you have the time. You will imbibe them with the elementals they represent, with words of your choice. I find that with this method, what works best is what you can come up with at the time. Prewritten words are not necessarily best. (I tend to do on-spot wording to most of my rituals and write them down later.) My favorite wording would go something like: "May the spirits of the realm of _____ bring forth from that world, a piece of it and may it be true to my purpose."

Again, wrap all of these things along with a small token into a packet. Charge it again, this time as a combined unit, and it is ready to use. The water element will have been sprinkled over the other contents before closing the packet. The salt will purify as the earth element, the ash represents the smoke from the incense (do not use new powder as it has not had smoke surround it yet) and finally the burned match, which, of course, represents the fire element. The sulphur has burned off, but its emanations remain and therefore can be seen as fire.

Have fun with your work. Don't see it as a chore if you can help it. There will be times when someone you know needs you to do work for them or their loved ones, but be sure to do the sort of work that you are relaxed with. If you are truly weary, put it off until the next day. Perhaps after a good night's sleep, you will be more able to do the thing properly.

Candle spells are common among Craftsmen and Craftswomen. There are different methods for this and you are free to develop your own. The much-used method (inscribing a candle with your goal in an economy of words and charging it) is the basis of most candle magic. The color of the candle and the time it takes to burn are important factors. The candle spells have the advantage of making use of the fire and air elements, both of which are carriers of your wishes.

Another method of spelling by candle is the thread and candle spell. In this you charge the candle and then inscribe your wish into it. Take a length of appropriately colored thread and wrap it around the candle until it is used up. With each revelation around the candle, state your intentions and visualize plainly your desire. When this has been done, burn the candle all the way down. When the candle is gone, take the ring of now-waxed thread and place it in a dark piece of cloth. Tuck it away and when the spell has worked, dispose of it in the usual way. I find that the best candles for this work are the small tea candles used in pot-pourri burners. It would not effect the spell if you used it in a burner until it is gone. The thread is left in a perfect circle at the bottom of the little aluminum dish.

There are some spells that a witch knows from the outset will not work. For instance, my mother suffers from chronic kidney failure and has dialysis three times a week to keep her alive. She has no kidney function whatever, and her kidneys could not be restored. Rather than try healing spells on the kidneys themselves, I concentrate on sending her energy on a daily basis. I also do work so that she may enjoy a relatively pain-free time. When she has had a particularly hard run on the machine that day, I will do a candle spell to try to increase her energy so she may enjoy her dinner and evening. This is what I am able to do. She knows that I do these things for her and she is grateful for the help and love that I—and my friends—send her way. If she has had a long spell of pain and weakness, I will equip her room with a candle burning constantly. She dislikes it at these times if the candle runs out. She enjoys seeing it there and takes comfort in the fact that it is lit in love.

If you are faced with the problem of feeling helpless, try every method you know. If these don't seem appropriate, then perhaps you could devise something which would ease a person who is ill, or cheer a person who is going through a rough time. Giving up is not a trait that I have run into among Wiccans. We are healers and as such, we are responsible to the folks who come to us to try everything in our power. We are not a religion of quitters but rather, we look at a situation from many angles and decide what might work. We try it and if it does not achieve the goal, we try something else. With the wide variety of methods and things to use, there is never a reason to give up. You never know when the answer will strike.

Candle Spell

> Candle burning bright and clear
> heed the words I spell
> take them to the Goddess
> whose love we know so well.
> I chant the wish I want tonight
> in strong tones ever be
> the Goddess grants the spells with love
> and sends these things to me.[3]

Here is the wording to Patricia Crowther's Water Spell. I find the words not only enchanting, but relevant for most needs.

> By Astral light, by moon-beams bright,
> I charge the water clear,
> To turn the tide for this your child,
> The face reflected here.
>
> The moon will take away all strife,
> Commence another phase—
> A mirrored surface, smooth as glass,
> Will thus describe your days.

---

[3]This is a spell I use that I wrote a number of years ago.

With hope serene within your breast,
Forget all hurt and pain.
Emerge from oceans newly born
And laugh at life, again.[4]

A Cauldron Spell for Prosperity

A dear friend of mine talked to me one day about doing a Circle for additional income by work being made available. We were both in rather dire circumstances at the time, so I devised this ritual for the purpose of drawing more opportunity for work, therefore an increased income. We had no intention of spelling for free money, but rather, we wanted to work for it.

I cast the Circle in the usual way and consecrated the area, altar, and tools. As I summoned the Quarter Guards, I responded to the elementals of each realm, invoking them to the Circle to aid us in our work. As the use and need of money is an entirely physical condition, I felt that to bring together the elemental creatures could only serve to enhance the spell. I had a very positive feeling as I called them.

We toasted the Old Ones and got to work. On the altar we had, in addition to the usual items (we used white for the altar candles) the following:

2 green candles
2 squares of black cloth 7" × 7"
2 ties for the squares of cloth
2 new coins
4 drops patchouli oil

---

[4]Patricia Crowther, *Lid off the Cauldron* (York Beach, ME: Samuel Weiser, 1981), p. 57.

a pinch of pine needles
a pinch of black tea
a few pieces of finely chopped orange peel
a pinch of cinquefoil (five-finger grass)
1 pint of mint (for success)
our intentions (written on a 5" square of paper)

Keeping a clear visualization of our need, we chanted softly: "These coins and more will surely be, with work the money comes to me."

We took up the green candles and very smoothly rubbed patchouli oil into them with the third finger of our right hand. This finger is considered the prosperity finger in the folklore from many countries. With this action, we continued to chant the words until the oil had been rubbed in completely.

After we replaced the candles on the altar, we rubbed the oil on our hands thoroughly into them. Hands are the receivers of the money and the patchouli would act as a reinforcement. The green candles would be burned later in our own homes, as this would charge the atmosphere and act as a magnet for the spell.

We then prepared the cauldron by lining it with our wish written on the square of paper. The two pieces of black material were laid out on the altar and the two coins were placed in the center of each. These coins had been resting on the pentagram for charging. The coins were sprinkled with water and so was the square of material. We took up each herb and sprinkled a little on the coins and a little over the messages in the cauldron. As we did each thing, we repeated our chant. When all of the herbs had been placed, we fastened the packets closed and meditated on our goal. This done, we replaced the completed packets on the altar.

We took our time passing our hands over the cauldron, chanting all the while. Taking up long fireplace matches, we lit the contents of the cauldron, and drew in the smoke of the cauldron through our hands. We let it surround us and we concentrated on the chant. The scent from this smoke was not at all unpleasant as mint and orange are nice. We continued to meditate for a time and then closed the Circle. We went our separate ways to light the green candles.

This spell is rather complicated in its equipment, but worth every fuss. We had only one goal to work on that evening and so the spell was designed to focus as much as possible. It worked and is still working. I have used it again and it does not fail. Allow your imagination and logic to work in connection with your spells and you will make powerful magic.

Color Guide

The elements each have a color which is representative of that particular realm. These should be used, or at the very least, kept in mind, whenever you are working with the elements themselves. They are helpful in visualization as you call up the Quarter Guards, as well. They are: red (fire), yellow (earth), blue (air) and green (water). They may not seem to physically correspond to the actual properties of the elements (blue theoretically should be used for water), but the appearance of discrepancy is understood by learned witches. The following list should prove helpful.

Black: corresponds to the Cabala at Binah (or Compassion) and shows dominion over the underworld. It is a color that absorbs all others, and many witches have extensive wardrobes of black. I find that to wear black when I am doing a psychic reading is helpful.

Blue: corresponds to the Cabala at Chesed (or Mercy). It is a color often used when trying to sort out emotional difficulties, such as impatience, anger, and jealousy.

Red: corresponds to the Cabala Geburah (or Strength). This is a color of force. Not a negative force but rather the kind of force used to fight psychic attack. Red is a color worn by many witches in the Mother stage of their lives. It is a color representing the blood of birth and is therefore full of the lifegiving fluids. Many witches will wear their red cords as a belt for a robe.

Green: corresponds to the Cabala Netzach (or Victory). This is a color rich in accomplishment and success. Mint green is a particularly good color for a success-oriented work. It is also the color most witches associate with spells for prosperity.

Yellow: corresponds to the Cabala Tiphareth (or Beauty). It is a color which gives off a tremendous vibration and should be worn when feeling low or tired.

Reddish-brown: corresponds to the Cabala Malkuth (or the Lower Kingdom). This, of course, does not imply the underworld, but rather the physical world that surrounds us. When needing to be your most alert in the mundane world, this is the color used.

Gold and **Silver**: have had some argument from different traditions. The two are both colors that correspond to the

Cabala Kether (or the Godhead). They are represented in Wicca as the Sun and Moon. Often, a male witch will wear gold for the God aspect and a female witch will wear silver for the Goddess aspect. I wear both. I have come to terms with my animus and I feel very comfortable representing both God and Goddess in my personal tastes. Silver and gold have long been considered sacred colors and they continue to be so. Their value on the world market shows their value in the physical world, as well. They are beautiful in the light of the candles in Circle and they let off the most spectacular emanations.

This is a general outline of the basic colors we deal with. Most witches have a cord of each for spell work. Color learning is greatly dependent on the intuitive powers of the witch and the traits of the various colors must be experienced to be understood. By this I mean that the colors must be used to be known. It is as simple as that. A novice can be handed a certain color cord, but without direction, that witch will not grasp the deep relation between the color of the cord and its use.

Chapter Four

CLAIRVOYANCE, SCRYING, AND DIVINATION

The art of "seeing" has been known as long as humans have had a spiritual existence. In the Ancient world, there were oracles, shamans, gypsies and mystics. Humankind has tried throughout its development to reach the world beyond what could be tasted, smelled, and touched. People felt in their hearts that something lay beyond, and witches use the Circle as a place to contact that world. The Circle is not necessary, but it provides a place of strength and love which makes the work a bit easier.

The *sight* is the ability to "know things." It happens to everyone at some level, but those who are non-believers will fail to recognize it. They put it down to "coincidence." Sight has often been referred to as intuition. Everyone has that little voice that may agree or disagree with the behavior of the self, but unless we are aware of it, we tend to ignore it. This voice never lets us down. Many believe that the little voice is a combination of intuition, spiritual guidance, and psychic strength.

Scrying is the use of darkened water or a dark looking-glass to see events or triggers. The easiest-found dark mirror is the kind with the back silver paint exposed and removed. The back can be painted with flat black paint and this will darken the mirror. I have found through past experience that some new witches get somewhat frightened the first few times they try scrying—especially when using a dark glass. Those with a natural ability do not get disturbed, but those trying to build their ability, have had some bizarre experiences. I have coached them through the fright, but it takes time to develop. When using a cauldron of water, I prefer to darken the water with water-soluble black or navy ink.

These surfaces (mirrors, water) give the witch a pool which can be gazed into without harm to the eyes. It has a soothing effect on the experienced scryer. The bottom does not show, and this gives the surface the appearance of an "endless" viewing space. The pictures do not appear on the glass or water, but rather the glass enables the witch to see these things more clearly in the psyche.

I often use my white cauldron and fill it with colored water. The color depends on the mood of the sight and on my personal preference. I generally use vegetable food coloring, if I am going to color the water something other than black. I find that the water-soluble inks of different colors are not deep enough, whereas food coloring has a deep rich tone if used properly. I use colors when I am seeking very specific information. For instance, I used deep blue when a client asked me about the cruise she and her husband were taking. I could clearly see the ship in the midst of the blue "ocean." Another time, I used green/blue when I was trying to gain insight into the property that a client was considering as a purchase. This property has a pond located on it, and the green/blue color gave me the local perspective for that particular piece of land.

I enjoy the use of herbs as a method for releasing psychic ability. The way I do this is to choose the herbs according to their gender and deity relationship. Certain herbs have divine patrons whose realm is psychic potentiality. Without crushing them, I take the herbs and gently mix them into a large bowl. After they are mixed, I shake them out onto a white cloth or paper and examine them. I see what has fallen together, the pattern (like tea leaves), the height of the piles of herbs, the evenness of the layout, etc. From this, my psyche is given a clear and accurate base from which to work. Clients enjoy this type of reading because they find it different.

Tarot cards are another useful tool in the art of divination. They are one of the richest sources of symbolism available. They correspond to the elements, the Cabala, the planets and their movements, and the directionals. They are varied, and the psychic using them must adopt whatever method and style is best on an individual basis. The Tarot and its interpretation, as well as the literature available, is vast and anyone wanting to begin study is in for a treat and a task. It would be impossible to tell you all there is to know about the cards here, but the secrets of the deck are well worth learning.

Many avenues of meditation and occult study unfold as you develop your ability. Patricia Crowther, in her book *Lid off the Cauldron*, talks about using the four elements with the cards. The method was shown to her by a Gypsy woman and since I have incorporated it into my readings, the method has unfailingly proved its worth. The woman shuffled the deck first by turning the cards over as a spade turns the earth, then dropped them one by one onto the table as raindrops. She then divided the deck into two and hit one pile against the other to create wind, and finally she fanned them out to reflect in the fire and release the sparkle. Ms. Crowther seemed delighted with this manner of bringing the cards to life. She wrote that they shone with an inner glow.[1]

The most important thing to remember when doing this exercise is that you need to really feel the elements when you represent them in the physical movement. Remember, for witches, movement is a dancing prayer.

As far as reading for clients is concerned, *psychometry* is the best method for me. Over the years, I have been able to develop this gift to a point where the cards, stones, or other methods are merely bonus. They enrich and enhance what I pick up from a personal item belonging to the client. At the moment, I work hard to filter my psychic receptions because I am involved in a number of writing projects, and a newsletter. My mind develops ideas at the darndest times and I must be conscious of what is received. This happens especially in the period when I am writing poetry. This can be annoying, but I take it as the Goddess sending me small gifts in the form of ideas, so I don't complain. A poem or recitation, because of its meter, will stay in the mind of its creator, trying out new bits. The best way to alleviate this is to immediately write it down so that I may let it go for the moment and go back to it later. I generally have paper and pen beside me at all times.

After working with novice witches and clients wanting to learn psychometry, I have developed a system whereby the touch becomes incredibly sensitive to vibrations and psychometric reading is possible. Please keep in mind that as you go through the exercises that follow, you must be free of distractions and influences. It takes hard

---

[1]Patricia Crowther, *Lid off the Cauldron* (York Beach, ME: Samuel Weiser, 1981) pp. 109, 110.

work and time to develop any psychic gift if you do not have an automatic talent for it.

Developing Psychometric Touch

When you work with this method you will use both a candle and a piece of crystal that has been stored in the freezer for a time. It doesn't matter in what order you do this, but remember, it will take several times to distinguish between the heat of the flame or cold of the rock and the vibrations emitted. You will eventually know which you are picking up, but as with all learning, it takes time. Be patient with yourself, and follow the instructions spelled out as follows.

Sit quietly in a semi-dark room with a table in front of you. Place the candle or crystal on a piece of white cloth on the table. White cloth is used because it will reflect rather than absorb energy. Place your hands on either side of the object, far enough away so that they feel nothing. Rest your arms on the table and get comfortable, because you must now focus. Take deep breaths and then exhale completely. Continue to breathe your Self into the relaxed and receptive Alpha state.[2] Focus your attention on the palms of your hands and completely slip into this spot. Feel— and imprint on your mind—what the palms of your hands do or do not feel. Remain focused on this for a good length of time. The longer you can maintain this, the better the next try will be.

Now move your hands together just a little. Do the palms of your hands feel the same? Make note of any

---

[2]Beta is the daily state of conscious awareness, whereas the Alpha state is achieved by deep breathing and slow counting until awareness of the physical body becomes secondary.

change in your mind or have someone who is assisting you write down impressions you have. Continue to move your hands a bit closer and note the sensations you feel. Do this until you either have felt only the temperature, or are weary. I cannot give you any detailed description of what you will experience when you are drawing vibration or energy rather than just feeling the temperature (heat or cold). The change is subtle, so you must keep an eye on it. But I guarantee that you will know. Awareness comes with practice and patience. Psychic abilities are no different from any other learning pursuit. They take time.

After you feel that you have experienced the vibratory output of the object, practice on everyday items from people around you. This will develop your ability further, and you will gain insight into the variety of emanations that come from different objects.

The hardest time that beginners seem to have is distinguishing their own thoughts from the psychic data that they receive. This, too, comes with practice. It may be frustrating at first but keep at it. You will find that one day, all is going well and you can relax with it.

Psychic work is a must for anyone interested in the occult sciences, no matter the path. *Visualization* is the "psychic architecture." Your psyche must take in information that your conscious mind feeds it and build a picture of what is required. It takes focus and stamina. You may find yourself feeling tired after particularly stressful sessions, but this is normal. Expect to weary from that exertion, deal with it, and come to understand the concept of expenditure/absorbtion.

There are many ways to rejuvenate yourself and to draw energy from around you. You can try something as simple as a walk. Breathe deeply as you go. The inhalation and exhalation of breath is an exchange of energy. It is continuous, so we don't always breathe as deeply as we should. The shallow breathing that we do only serves to frustrate the body because we do not fill our lungs and we do not take in enough throughout the day. So breathe, breathe, breathe!

Another method of rejuvenation is to take a bath. The water element is one of the most soothing to both the physical and astral bodies. We literally merge with the water as we sink into the tub. Our bodies are made up of an incredible amount of water and by surrounding our-selves with it, we can feel our bodies become one with the elemental spirits of that realm. Close your eyes, relax, and breathe! Draw energy from the water that surrounds you. It gives comfort and warmth. We come into this world from a watery environment and we can return to the secu-rity of that place for a short time. Add the other three elements by lighting a candle near you, burning incense, and throwing a little seasalt into your bath water.

To dispel negative energy, hold a crystal or stone (pro-vided it is special to you) between the palms of your hands. Visualize the negativity flowing into the stone through your hands. The stone will not be harmed, as the exchange of positive and negative energies is what the Mother does best. Earth is a living organism and it draws energy to, and releases it from itself. Stones are an exten-sion of the Mother. They can be purified by holding them under cold running water for a while. If you do not have a stream or lake near you that you can put your stones into, then you can use domestic water supplies. Please reuse the water. Run the water over the stone into a bowl, and keep picking it up and pouring again. When you are fin-ished, place the container of water on your altar for a few days. If you hold a Circle, cleanse and purify it then. It may now be used for other purposes. Don't waste. I have not had a plant suffer from being watered with my recycled water, and I know that my powers as a witch are able to purify plain water in spite of the negativity. Some may criticize my practice, but I know, as well as any witch who is environmentally aware, that there is just not enough water to continue wasting it. We must all do what we can to reduce our water usage and reuse when we are able. That is why I suggested a bath for rejuvenation. If a shower is taken for basic cleansing, then, yes, take a shower. These showers use less water than it takes to fill the tub. If you use a shower for the purpose of rejuvenation, chances are pretty good that you will want to stand there for some time. The water feels wonderful, but please use a bath for this purpose, as in the long run, it takes less water.

Witches do have an advantage, because by means of power and ritual, we are able to purify something when we wish. Some things may take some time, while others may take repeated effort. The water to cleanse the stone a witch has used is not unclean, per se, but rather, its positive and negative energies have become unbalanced. By placing it on the altar for a time, balance can be restored. The altar of a witch's home is the most balanced place available. Let your altar work for you and the Mother. Your plants will thrive on this water because not only has the balance been restored, but it has been recharged as well!

Let the critics complain. In this time of environmental pulling-together, witches—as children of the Goddess—must do their part in paring down the usages. If we do, then perhaps more will follow suit. We are the pagans, the people of the Mother, Her children. We must be aware! We can show our love for Her by providing a balanced and clean environment for the children to come. I do not consider my reuses "sloppy magic." On the contrary, they follow the Wiccan Rede, and harm none. Be conscious of Her gifts and use them wisely. We will have other lifetimes to spend here so we'd best take care today.

YOUR BOOK OF SHADOWS

Today the Wiccan researcher has many Books of Shadows available to them. These books are rich and alive with the basic ideas and goals of the Craft. Many writers have contributed their knowledge and Books either in part or in their entirety. These writings all add to the growing wealth of information which can be found today. There have been arguments in the past over which Book was valid or not valid, copied correctly or incorrectly, and so on. These arguments have, at times, become petty and waste valuable time. Yes, it would be grand if we had a Book of Shadows that the Wiccan world knew to be an original text of quite an age. There are two reasons why this just cannot be so.

First, there is the forgery. It would be hard to prove the age of material within an ancestral line, as the truth or validity of the document is known only by members of the family. And even the family has lost generations of kinfolk who could verify it. I know that there are probably many traditional witch families who believe their information to be old and accurate. I would dearly love to possess such a Book. However, I believe that they are extremely rare.

The second reason is purely an evolutionary one. Our traditions go back many thousands of years. Our roots are the roots of the earth-based folk. We all come from people who tended the farms and agriculture was the way of life. Rarely have I heard a witch say that their ancestral line was that of royalty or aristocracy. There are, I am sure, some Wiccans who do hail from the wealthier lines but they appear to be few. And let us face the fact that most farm folk were not necessarily illiterate, but rather, had neither the time nor knowledge to write down all magical notions. The people who were educated were the church clergy and their apprentices. Those who could read and write Latin or local languages were busy copying texts for the Church. Many may have been practicing pagans but few would put their positions in jeopardy by becoming scribes for the Craft. It was a matter of personal safety and not a disloyalty to our ways.

There is a third factor involved here as well. There may, indeed, have been a number of "diaries" or journals of witches. Many may have written the herbal remedies for future use. However, through the "burning times," many of these books would likely have been confiscated and destroyed. And of course, such material would have been used as evidence against the witch. So it remains highly unlikely that documentation has survived.

Much of the surviving Craft knowledge has been passed through generations by observation and memory. It is only in recent times that the Books of Shadows of other witches have been available. The earliest one we have is the Gerald Gardner book. Doreen Valiente has authenticated his work and has been able to find the certificates that prove his stories of his own teacher and his own initiation into the Craft. She had a long search but eventually found the documentation to substantiate Gardner's claim to being initiated by a New Forest witch named Dorothy Clutterbuck.[1]

Many contemporary witches have added to the beautiful seasonal festivals that are the basis of the Craft. We have wonderful tools and accents to adorn our altars and many good writings to follow for ritual. Many of us write our own and all the additions have merit and value. Ceremonial magical practices have emerged in many traditions of the Craft and, as with everything else, if they are positive and add to your work then they are welcome. Your work must be performed in a deeply aware state.

Sometimes we need to remember that additional tools of all kinds—good though they may be—are not necessary to the practice of the Craft. This is why witches (or students) who come to me are encouraged to hug trees, sit on the grass, wade in a stream, and perform rituals outdoors (if possible) using very little equipment. Though our tools lend themselves to indoor working and enhance our state in Circle, they are not essential. With nothing, or with a wand from a tree, a handful of earth, a bowl of water, and a candle, we can build a natural Circle which can induce an incredible awareness of the Mother and of ourselves. Every once in a while we need to experience the simplicity of just such a Circle.

I will not include in this chapter the wording of my own Book of Shadows. Or rather, the opening to my original book. This is available from other authors in a more pure form. I come from the Celtic lines with many changes in custom and the work that I used as a novice is basically the same as the British writers Crowther, the Farrars, and Sanders—although having been in the Craft so long, the

---

[1]Janet Farrar and Stewart Farrar, *A Witches Bible*, Volume 2 (New York: Magickal Childe, 1981), p. 283. If you don't have this book, the current version is called *The Witches Bible Compleat*.

wording for Ritual and Ceremony is now almost always my own. The wording for this tradition has been fine-tuned by Doreen Valiente for the Farrars' *A Witch's Bible*.[2] She was an initiate of Gardner, himself, and has added much to the knowledge of the Gardner Book.

This is not to say that my Book is any less a witch's book, merely because it has withstood the passage from Britain to Canada, but also because of its use by those along the way. Obviously, if there are changes from the original, then these, in fact, are fingerprints of the witches from whom it has passed. I have compared the openings from my own and the Gardner version and have found that the essence is the same. I use as an example the often referred to charge that Gardner was "obsessed with ritual scourging." I for one do not particularly care for the manner in which the scourge is discussed in the original documents. I find that the changes have come about in a manner which suggest personal preference. But regardless of how another witch might judge my Book of Shadows, it is full of well-worked methods, recipes, rituals, poetry, and magical work. It is the record of my years as a witch. Even my earliest diaries appear like a Book of Shadows, interspersed with girlhood imaginings. I have been writing esoteric poetry and rituals for as long as I can remember.

The Book should be as much a part of you as your own body. You do not have to write like an author to maintain a Book. Write what you want and feel. The Book is for your eyes only. When I initiate witches, they copy only the opening works—the work that I myself copied. The rest, if I desire, is not for other eyes. I do not object to passing on certain rituals or spells that I have written but only to

---

[2]Janet Farrar and Stewart Farrar, *A Witches Bible Compleat* (New York: Magickal Childe, 1984). See the Book of Shadows in this book, which is also Volume 2 of *A Witches Bible*.

people that I know can handle the responsibility. Obviously I trust those I have initiated, but I find it difficult when a witch that I have recently met expresses interest in my journal of magic. As with all magical tools or things we use, we are protective of them because for us, they hold great power. And with a power that potent, it stands to reason that we would want to ensure purity of motive before opening ourselves, our work, or our books to another.

In my Book I also record information regarding my magical work that is unsuitable for the novice and would serve only to confuse. It pertains to the results of certain rituals or spells, descriptions of divinations I have performed, etc. My Book contains information regarding the queries and problems that people come to me about and the progress they make. This is personal and I would not share client information with anyone. The names of clients are never used, and the problems they share with me are for no other eyes. Witches like myself who do a great deal of spiritual counseling maintain client confidentiality like any other professional counselor.

In addition, I record work which the student would not know what to do with and thus could backfire. Therefore, a person holding a third degree[3] will recognize the importance of withholding some parts of our Books of Shadows. It is not that we are a secret society, but rather, like any teaching, there should be a certain order in which the novice receives information.

The Book of Shadows is called thus not because of any evil or dark words within it, but because its contents enable a Wiccan to pass through the mists or shadows to

---

[3]Many wiccan traditions hold to a three degree learning process, whereby the novice is presented with knowledge appropriate for his or her level.

the magical lands. The Book represents all of the potential of the Craft in relation to the individual witch. The words inside give guidance, peace, motivation, and learning. The Book is a Journal of Magical Pursuits and Philosophy. It is a book of spells, chants, rituals, and poetry that have proven their effectiveness over time. It contains no evil if it belongs to a member of the Craft. It is a book of positive deeds. If we use the definition of the word "bible" from the Oxford Dictionary—authoritative book—The Book of Shadows is very much a bible for the witch that has written it. Janet and Stewart Farrar have entitled their two-volume set *A Witches Bible*, and, as yet, I have heard no objections to it.

Aside from the opening passages which are available to anyone, here are some passages and works from my Book which I feel could be valid contributions to a Wiccan library. Many entries in my Book are works of friends and colleagues in the Craft which have been passed to me or that I have read in a published copy, but the bulk of the book is written by me for my needs or the needs of the people I work with. These perhaps can be of assistance to those who find writing difficult and who seek wording for some rituals and works.

Ritual for Healing

"Gentle Goddess, send our guardian Michael to fulfill our hopes and fill our brother/sister with strength. Allow we, your children to direct our power to _____ and heal the wounds within."

Facing south, raise your athame

"Michael, mighty guardian of this our physical plane, send out your great warriors to dispel the fear of our friend, and with a slash of your great sword, renew this weakened body to health."

"Great Lady, love _____ and enfold him/her in your arms to nourish from your life-giving breasts. Let us keep you forever in our hearts. So Be It."

Ritual for Naming a Sword

When a Wiccan friend of mine finally decided on the sword he wanted, he came to me and asked if I would name it and present it in Circle to him. I thought this sounded delightful and agreed. We had the sword shipped to my home so that he would not see it until the actual presentation. I wrote the following ritual for the occasion and hope that it will be of help to any who need it.

The movements are really up to those involved, but I did blindfold him until the end of the wording. He later told me that to listen to my voice without seeing anything brought him a feeling of mystery and he felt more able to concentrate on what was being said. Here is the ritual.

"I consecrate this sword with water so it may be at one with the Lady of the Lake. May she smile upon it. Strength and virtue will she invest in it. So Mote It Be.

"I consecrate this sword with air. Air is the element of phantasms and spirits. The sword of _____ will indeed direct those of air. So Mote It Be.

"I consecrate this sword with the salt of the earth. Earth, where its metals were born. Born deep in the caverns and recesses of the Mother. So Mote It Be.

"I consecrate this sword with fire. Fire is the element of its being. It will represent the element of fire for all eternity. It is forged with fire, and will be formidable in the works of the Craft. Let it truly represent fire in the mind of your priest _____. So Mote It Be."

The Presentation

"I present to you this sword which has been duly consecrated. May you always use it with peace and love in your heart. Use it in the names of (Goddess name) and (God name).

"The sword shall be known by the element which serves it. Child of the Goddess, from this day forward, this sword shall be known by the name _____."

Ritual of Wrapping the Heart

This is a solemn and powerful ritual when used for someone in need of very positive energy. It does not mean that this is a healing spell, but rather it is a revitalization spell. It must be done with two or more people as there are actions required within the ceremony itself.

Use white cords to ensure purity of purpose. The requestor is seated in the center of the Circle facing the altar, hands folded across the heart, right over left. The end of the cord belongs in the left palm, closest to the heart. Wrap requestor with the cord around the chest at the level of the heart, doesil. Visualize while wrapping the intent of the request for help.

See the person clearly in your mind. If you are not associated with the recipient of the power, focus on the name, or other familiar aspect. The end of the cord should be tucked into place for the duration of the ritual.

The requestor remains in this posture, with eyes closed, intent on the person for whom the request has been made. He/she should envision this person connected to him/her by the wrapped white cord. The clearer this picture can become, the greater the spell. The priest (or priestess) assisting in the rite stands before the altar, arms raised in the Goddess position. The following words are recited:

"Oh, Great Lady, Mother of us all, hear us. Come meet with your children. Caer Arianrod holds the power. Let the veil be penetrated and our work be done.

"This cord is the silver cord of life. The heart gives birth to the power within. The cord carries light and love to _____, your child on Earth. May our love stream forth along the cord from the heart of the Circle to the heart of the one in need. Goddess, hear us. So Mote It Be."

Lift the cord over the person's head after a time of intense meditation on the purpose. Knot the cord one time only, and wrap it in a piece of black cloth. Keep it tucked away for one full cycle of the Moon to ensure all aspects of the Goddess.

Chapter Six

THE CHARGE
OF THE GODDESS

There are many translations and variations of the "Charge of the Goddess." The Charge that I have in my Book of Shadows most closely resembles the version which Janet and Stewart Farrar have published in their book *A Witches Bible*, Volume 1, *The Rituals*.[1] There are some changes which have occurred but generally it is the same. My friend has a copy and the wording of the translation is quite different again. My version was obtained while copying my Shadows. This is the one I will use here, because it is the prettiest I have read, and because it is, after so many years of use, a part of me.

Also note that Doreen Valiente has written a most stunning version of the Charge in poetry form.[2] It is well worth reading and is a moving, lovely piece.

[1]Janet Farrar and Stewart Farrar, *A Witches Bible*, Volume 1 (New York: Magickal Childe, 1981), pp. 42, 43.

[2]Doreen Valiente's version of the Charge is discussed in Janet and Stewart Farrars' book *A Witches Bible*, Volume 1 (New York: Magickal Childe, 1981), p. 42.

The Charge

"These are the words of the Goddess:

"Whenever ye have need of anything and once in a month, and better it be when the Moon is full, then shall ye assemble in a magical place and adore the spirit of me, who am Queen of all Witches. There shall ye assemble, ye who are fain to learn all witchery, yet have not won its deepest secrets; to these will be thought, and taught things that are yet unknown.

"Ye shall be free from bondage; ye shall dance, sing, feast, make music and love all in my praise. For mine is the ecstasy of the spirit, and mine is also joy on earth; for my law is love unto all beings.

"Keep pure your highest ideals; strive ever toward them; let naught stop you or turn you aside. For mine is the Secret Door which opens upon the Land of Youth, and mine is the Cup of the wine of Life, and the Cauldron of Cerridwen, which is the holy Grail of Immortality.

"I am the Gracious Goddess, who gives the gift of joy unto the hearts of men. Upon earth I give the knowledge of the spirit eternal; and beyond death, I give peace and freedom, and reunions with those who have gone before. Nor do I demand sacrifice; for behold, I am the Mother of all living, and my love is poured upon the Earth.

"I, who am the green earth, and the white Moon, the mystery of the waters and the desire of the spirit, call unto your soul. Arise and come unto me.

"Let my worship be within the heart, for behold all acts of love are my rituals. Therefore, let there be beauty and strength, power and compassion, honor and humility, mirth and reverence within you.

"And you who think to seek for me, know thy seeking will avail thee not, unless thou knowest the mystery; if that which thou seek thou find not within thee, thou will never find it without thee.

"For behold, I have been with ye from the beginning and I am that which is attained at the end of desire.

So speaks the Goddess."

Drawing Down the Moon

For most witches I have talked to, the Charge is a very important event in Circle because as a High Priestess recites this piece, she feels the Goddess in her. The Drawing Down of the Moon is the actual entrance of the Goddess into the Circle, but the Charge is the time when the Priestess loses herself for a moment and the light of the Lady shines through her eyes. She is fired with the spirit of all that is the Goddess. At that moment she is capable of extraordinary power and love.

I enjoy following the Charge with the Witches Rune. However, if I have an hands-on healing to do for someone, I prefer to do this directly after the Charge, mainly because the power of the Goddess is directly in my fingertips and most potent at that moment.

If I am working without a High Priest, then often I will perform a solo Drawing Down. I wrote this when I moved to a new province and was working by myself. Perhaps it will be of use to those sisters in the Craft who must work alone.

Drawing Down the Moon—Solo

After the Circle is cast, all is consecrated, and the Watchtowers invoked, the solo priestess stands in front of the altar with her arms outstretched (as opposed to the Osiris position; this one helps the witch to feel herself opening to the spirit of the Goddess) and repeats:

> I call the Mighty Mother of us all,
> bringer of life and love.
> By life and love do I ask thee to descend upon your Priestess _____.

Use the invoking pentagram and repeat:

> The Goddess is with me. She and I are one. Her light will shine through the eyes of this child of Her womb.

Limitless Potential

As with any spiritual system, Wicca is understood through the knowledge of its parts. Only then can a full and rich spiritual harmony exist. The Dancing Prayer of Wicca is a passage to the "Whole." The spirituality of this path is contained within its three foundational parts. With these three characteristics of a Wiccan's belief system, the universe unfolds and new knowledge nourishes our daily lives. Use these three manifestations with love in your heart and you will find your life is enriched beyond comprehension.

TABLE OF LIMITLESS POTENTIAL

MAGIC: opportunity for limitless potential
FAITH: awareness of limitless potential
WORSHIP: expression of limitless potential

Worship is the mover and shaker of the group. Worship is the expression through ritual, meditative communication, dance, love, prayer, and all those things that "end up" expressing your deepest beliefs. I say "end up" because often we will go into ritual or another method without being totally open to the idea of what we are doing. When given a chance, whatever the method, we often find ourselves relating to the experience, so that Worship, once again, is the final factor.

A young friend of mine who participates regularly in seasonal festivals once described Wicca as a Dancing Prayer. No matter what form Worship takes, it is the essence behind it which causes it to be filled with graceful energy.

Because I worship my faith daily and sometimes without premeditation, I neglected to include a section on it in the first draft of this book. It is so much a part of me that without it, I would be merely a shell, existing on oxygen only. I do not suggest that I do circles constantly or ritual all the time. On the contrary, premeditation is an enhancing factor in ritual.

Rather, I refer to the daily uses of the Craft that open my heart to the experience of the moment. For example, I hear of a friend with a bad cold. If asked, I will suggest safe, medicinal herbs which will relieve the symptoms of a cold. I will then either light a candle (with meaningful/ small incantation), prepare a healing pouch, grace my altar with a healing stone or burn healing herbs. Sometimes, if my immediate circumstances prohibit any of these ways, I will close my eyes and visualize one of them. In this way, I become connected to the person who is ill, and I am able to send positive, healthy energy. By using the Table of Limitless Potential, I become aware of the opportunity to see this person in glowing health, to understand that this person has the potential for glowing health, and I can express that which will cause the glowing health of that person.

As a devoted and practicing Wiccan, I use worship to enhance my heartfelt concentration, motives, and end results. I feel joy in my heart when I know I am doing all I can do. When an animal has been struck down on the road, it is automatic for me to ask that the Goddess take it safely to its place in the Summerlands. In this way, I feel that at least one person (me) has acknowledged the life of that animal. Many who pass it, acknowledge the death of the creature. As a Wiccan and believer in many lives, I must make myself continually aware of life and its pure opposite—death.

My faith gives me strength, hope, love, responsibility, and joy. These are big pluses in any spiritual growth. The Table of Limitless Potential gives me a sense of really contributing. It forces me to look at life with a smile. If I see each "down time" as an opportunity to learn, then that time will seem less severe. I try to find something to laugh about daily. Ours is a household of silliness and the ridiculous.

This may sound childlike and trite. However, being a witch gives me joy beyond explanation. I see the world as a veritable smorgasbord of opportunity. Life is too short not to see it this way. Even the painful aspects become increasingly important to my growth cycle. Those events which cause me grief and sorrow have limitless potential to show us that these things are a part of the greater whole. I will mourn for a loved one, but at the same time, I realize that these are tests of my faith and personal courage and power. If I can pass through each test and come out a stronger person, then I am fulfilling my little part in the Cosmic Tapestry.

Blending with the Mundane

Witches, like everyone else, have to acknowledge and eliminate those habits which cause us to exert negative behavior. Simply put, all these habits or insecurities are caused by—or occur—in direct result of something that belongs to our physical existence.

For example, a friend recently had a terrifying experience in which she found herself having flashbacks of very violent experiences. Because she knew they were memories, she started to exhibit negative behavior in the form of nailbiting, overeating, not sleeping, and personal disfunctioning.

Her need to clarify the experiences of her childhood were overwhelming. She finally started to trust herself and open a dialogue to her Inner being. She understood that these occurrences were not her doing and over a long period of time was able to realize that she was still alive, she had her health, and had people who cared for her. She allowed herself (in controlled settings of her choosing, with friends available to support her) to experience each and every new memory. She knew she must open herself to these painful thoughts despite the fact that they were almost unbearable. If we tape a movie from the TV and watch it repeatedly, no matter how shocking it is, we will desensitize ourselves out of sheer survival instinct. Thus, the movie no longer has an impact on us.

She decided to deal with her memories on the same basis. Once she was able to face them without fear, she arranged with me to do a Rite of Release. With a ritual such as this, the participant is setting the stage for a deliberate and precise "letting go." We must allow this separation process in all instances—be they negative or positive. Anything left undone is unfinished business for later. We must take this opportunity to allow it the non-harmful place in our Selves to which it will go. With it safely tucked aside, we can direct our energies to things of the present which require our attention.

The worship of witches becomes more and more a part of us as we shed the veils of insecurity and fear.

Chapter Seven

TIME AWAY FROM RITUAL

Many people have asked me about periods of separation from the Craft that most practitioners and students experience. It very likely happens to anyone who participates in certain religions and beliefs. We all have to step back now and then to allow something we are involved in to take the center stage. Perhaps it is school for some, or family, a second job, career problems, or vacation times. These can all become impediments on our path of spirituality and practice.

But any Wiccans who must set aside the actual ritual and practice of Wicca know in their hearts that they feel none the less Wiccan for this. If people must take a separation for a period of time, there are ways that Wiccans handle this from inside the Craft.

Most witches that I have encountered take great satisfaction from a Circle well done. It gives them a feeling of accomplishment and security. Therefore, if witches must take time away from Craft work, then the following ritual of separation will help ensure that your Craft ties are not harmed because of any feelings of being separated from it. This ritual is not mandatory nor necessary. However, I wrote it when I needed to feel a direct connection during periods of time away. It worked for me and perhaps it can ease your psyche, too.

Cloaked in the Circle

This ritual should be done by a solo witch or working partnership. It is unsuitable for a group as the vibrancy of the ritual comes from the person who faces separation.

Cast your Circle in the method you regularly use, with the exception that when you invoke the Watchtowers, refrain from using a reference to the particular element that each contains within its realm. If you are working as two, then each can recite the lines. Or you can develop a workable and enjoyable ritual style based on the manner that has worked for you in the past.

Stand at your altar facing north. Raise the Pentacle high and meditate on its earth aspect. See clearly in your mind the earth and all Her bounty. See the creatures of the earth element. Use whatever will distinctly link you to this element. Clearly feel the earth in all her splendor. Feel Her darker side as well—the deep cool earth on which we stand. Feel this in your mind and through your body and recite as follows.

> Great Mother, you who is the mother of all living things.
> Of the creatures, all who are from you.
> I come as your child _____,
> bringing with me the joy and blessings of my heart.
> I feel the earth within me and about me,
> I know that if I must leave the sacred circle, you will be with me. And this will stay in my heart.
> So Be It.

Touch the Pentacle to your forehead (the third eye), and replace it on the altar. Move doesil to the east, with your burning censor. Recite:

> Great and mighty creatures of the East who bestow the gift of breath upon the world, hear me.
> I must leave the gentle Circle for a time.
> I know that in ought I do, you will be there.
> You, Sylphs of air, come and be with me on my journey in life. I breathe you into my heart.
> So Be It.

Gently breathe in some of the scent from your burner and feel its presence in you. Replace the censor on the altar.

Next you will take up your sword or athame, and move to the south quarter of your Circle. Point it straight into the air in front of you and repeat:

> Oh creatures of fire, hear me.
> I come to seek your assistance.
> Stay within me as I take this time away from the circle.
> I will retain your warmth and courage for my own.
> I seek to absorb the dance of your flame.
> Be in me and about me.
> So Be It.

Touch the flat of the blade to your third eye, keeping in mind the aspects of fire. Replace the blade on your altar.

And finally, take up your goblet of water and move to the west point of your Circle. Hold the goblet high in both hands. Repeat the following.

> Oh, mighty waters, essence of life in the womb of the Goddess.

Bring with you the soothing comfort,
the cool drink, the cleansing bath.
I must journey outward, beyond this Circle.
Be with me, stay with me.
Let the womb of the Lady surround me.
So Be It.

Take a deep drink of the water and feel it move through your body. Consciously imprint this in your mind. Take a drop on the end of your finger, and gently rub it into the place of your third eye. See the water clearly.

Stand in the middle of your Circle facing the altar. Raise your hands high and see the Divine Mother and Forest Father before you. Repeat:

I surround myself with you, Mighty Circle
that I may wear you as a cloak, my time away.
You will be with me and about me.
You will fold your elements around me and embrace
    me.
I am a child of the Goddess and in Her care I will stay.
I will call you forth from time to time,
to fill me with the power centered here.
This I ask in the name of [Goddess] and [God].
So Be It.

Kneel in the center of the Circle and envision the Circle shedding a second skin and enfolding itself around you. When you have a clear picture of this in your mind, absorb it. You should have a talisman that is of special significance to the occasion. At this time, consecrate it in the normal fashion and close the Circle. Do not forget to thank the Watchtowers for the gifts of the elements which you now wear.

You must remember that you are never really away from your Circle, as you can cast it any time or any place you may be. If your visualization of each step in the process is clear, the Circle around you will be as strong as at the Covenstead.

You will find, on your return, that you never were away. You will shed your temporary elemental cloak, let it merge with the Mother-Circle again, and raise your arms in joyous return. The cloak provided you with security and protection as you needed it, but now you may spread your altar and toast the Goddess for returning you to the safety of your own environment.

Chapter Eight

THE "SPOOKY" SIDE OF WICCA

Many non-witches view the Craft as "spooky." By that I mean that many draw their idea of what a witch is by the movies they see or the novels they read. I used to read horror novels. I find, however, that I am mellowing and have grown very tired of the continual brutality in many of them now. I find myself drawn to happier reads. One novel that I must admit struck me as well-researched in Wicca is a book by Whitley Strieber called *Cat Magic*.[1] As a novelist, he has ribboned the story with some horror and did twist a plot but his portrayal of witchcraft shows a remarkable level of understanding of what witches do, and why they conduct their lives as they do. He describes a covenstead with many covens working together in a way that many witches would love to belong to—a life outdoors, gardening and building, celebrating and healing. This way of life appeals to many pagans. We find the noise and hustle of the cities hard to take. We regularly tighten our grip on the cycles of the seasons. We have to. Our Sabbats and celebrations do this for us. They show us the

[1]Whitley Strieber, *Cat Magic* (London: Grafton Books, 1987).

time of year and what we look forward to. Even at Samhain, witches look forward to the darker days and nights of winter to increase inner learning, to work on things that require solitary ways, and to work around the home with writings or research. These months are marvelous for learning herbal work and candle magic. We usually keep many candles lit in the winter. The flame of the candle always gives us a sense of warmth and power.

Most witches who work in the public eye are accustomed to being seen as spooky. And there is a side to Wicca that is distinctly spooky! Many who come to the Craft like this aspect. The energy exuded from a woman or man scrying can be eerie. Wiccans are sometimes thought of as spooky because they tend to make eye contact with people and are able to hold it. Part of the teachings into third degree deal with the direct link to a person through his or her eyes.[2] I remember this teaching well and I gain an overwhelming understanding of someone as I link with them.

Many, however, who seek the Craft are envisioning witches in moonlit meadows or graveyards calling to the spirits of the other world to join them. Stirring pots of foggy brew, gazing without end into its depths; these are the images for some people. I have been asked what I was brewing when things have been cooking on the stove. Generally, I stick to the pat answer of lizards teeth and frog blood. (A deep apology to all lizards and frogs who I may offend!)

Many contemporary witches consider the "calling up of spirits" a non-Wiccan activity. Many feel that this interrupts the karma of the person that has passed. I am a long-time believer in the theories of reincarnation and karmic

---

[2]The third degree is the final level of knowledge in many wiccan traditions.

balance, but I do not see occasional spirit connection as a disruption of karma. I would never advocate continual practice of seancing. I feel that contact with a loved one is a precious gift that is not to be mistreated. But occasionally throughout the year, I will work to channel my spirit guide so that I may gain insight on a problem that is giving me more than a little trouble. By achieving knowledge or helpful intuitive confirmation, I am able to consider the problem from a different angle, thus developing a new way to deal with it. I do not consider myself disturbing another's karma, because I believe that if we are able to return to the physical plane for each lifetime, then we must surely have knowledge of it between incarnations. And if we have knowledge, then we may very well be able to communicate that to those still here. There are more than enough cases of spiritual activity that have withstood the attempts to disprove them. The transcripts from Jane Roberts' Seth, the Michael transcripts, the cases of automatic writing, and the incredible number of insights received by folks from the beyond, plus the numerous cases of familial linkage at time of death, cannot be discounted.

Karma enables us to co-exist with many different levels of being, and there are going to be times when these levels overlap. This causes us to experience "spooky" things. Witches experience these things in a different way. To us they are not spooky, but rather they are informative and act as a medium for knowledge. I, along with many other people, have felt a presence, heard noises, and have had communication from the etheric realm. We must examine these things and realize that perhaps those who communicate from beyond, do so as a choice. I have lifetimes worth of questions to be answered—like all human beings—and I will use whatever source is available. If I am able to communicate with one who can give me insight, I will listen. Perhaps this is spooky and perhaps not.

Aside from psychic perceptiveness and the relation-ship with the spiritual, there are still many spooky aspects to Wicca. Herbalists are often viewed as odd or mysteri-ous. The ingredients we use are not sold in bright flashy containers that catch your eye by force. They are not nationally advertised. We will probably never see a com-mercial for what we keep on our herb shelves. (Certainly not eye of newt!) Whether a witch is a medicinal herbalist or a scent herbalist, the glass jars you see on our shelves hold things like witch hazel, coriander, sandlewood, bur-dock, hyssop and many others. The labels are small and unobtrusive, and usually look more mysterious than they are. Not everyone may have the intuition that it takes to work herbal magic, but you can learn how, and with effort, you will succeed.

Last Samhain, I was alone at my house. My daughter had gone to her grandmother's and I had such a busy time that I had not felt like company for the festival. I had a celebration with my fellow Craftspeople a few days earlier and had gone to see a play about witches that I thoroughly enjoyed. I love the Wheel Festivals, but I do not insist on a mandatory date. My sabbats and esbats come as close as possible to the correct times, but they have to fit into my schedule as well.

While I sat alone that evening, I had the eeriest feeling that I was surrounded by many who had passed on. Samhain is, of course, the most psychically open time of the Wheel, when the veil is at its thinnest. The distance between the worlds lessens and many may pass back and forth between. I have had wonderful experiences with the Samhain Sabbat in the past, but never have there been so many with me at once. To facilitate this feeling, I darkened my home and lit candles. I donned a comfortable robe, lit incense and arranged a spot to sit on the rug. My home became "spooky" and I had a wonderful evening allowing those around me to interact with me. I love that sensation of feeling slightly eerie as opposed to so many who feel afraid. I sat comfortably and allowed their energy to move about me as I shifted between the worlds that night. I felt many different emotions given to me by those who came. It was a very educational experience.

The "spookiness" that people experience is caused by a shift in the mental thought processes of the people experiencing it. We actually think of a situation as spooky before we feel that familiar tingle up the spine. We look around and realize the circumstances are eerie and this is what creates the tingle. If you can manage to convert that eerie feeling into a curiosity rather than allowing it to develop into fear, then you may experience something and learn from it.

Some people only experience fear, and this imprints the face of the monster onto an otherwise harmless entity. If you can avoid this by opening yourself to it, then perhaps you will become more comfortable with the things around you that you can't taste, hear, feel, smell, or see. These five senses have limited our ability to accept the sixth, even though many of us have experiences that could not be explained by the five senses alone. Allow your feelings their freedom, rather than restricting their essence with fear.

Chapter Nine

THE WITCH EACH DAY

Wiccans are really very ordinary people. We come from all walks of life. Our careers are as different as the people who hold them. Some of us try to incorporate the Craft into our manner of making a living. Some write, some do psychic readings, some are herbalists, some do all of this and more. But at the same time, there are subtle differences that distinguish us from non-Wiccans.

Most witches I know have extensive libraries ranging from books on Wicca to philosophy. Sciences, religions of all kinds, and metaphysical volumes fill our bookshelves. Most of us are amateur historians and have a wide range of period information. Many have particular tastes in music. Most Wiccans love celtic, classical, and new age music, as well as having an open mind about other kinds of non-invasive sound.

We are drawn to environments of peace and tranquillity. We light candles very often; we have our houses scented most of the time, and we come into our homes, shedding the anxiety and costume of the work-a-day world. The timelessness of our homes is most welcoming.

Taking a moment to stand in the midst of that atmosphere that we have created, we breathe in the soothing love of the Goddess, and in so doing, once again absorb the private atmosphere of our home.

It is hard for some people to imagine how the Craft comes into view when talking about the mundane things we must do in life—like waiting in line at the bank, the supermarket, the gas station. Wiccans don't waste time standing in a line being frustrated by how long it is. They take a copy of a particular ritual they want to learn and read it. The better they know an incantation, the more dramatic the ritual will be. They learn the "hands free" approach to ritual by learning the pieces from their Shadows when they have a few minutes free. They learn as they copy the piece to take with them, and they learn by reading while standing in line or riding on a bus or subway.

Most Wiccans that I know have two things in common—candles and plants. Things grow in my home. I have full bookshelves and many interesting stones. But most of all, what I have is a good feeling space with sparks of light glowing softly most of the time and plants that grow despite my occasional neglect.

Witches tend to practice healing. We are not always aware that we are doing this. When we are around people, we draw negative energy away from them and ground it so that they may take in positive energy instead. We do this almost unknowingly. We are able to ground the negativity because the early training in the Craft has taught us this. This grounding is vital to everything that a witch does. If not, those who do psychic readings, spiritual counseling, and herbal magic would walk around continually absorbing negativity and not dispersing it. We must rid ourselves of it in order to function and do our work. This absorption and exhaustion of the nastier vibes is perhaps what makes people happy in our homes. They feel relaxed and worry-free. I have a few places in my home which function as altars. They may not necessarily look like altars, but to another Wiccan, that is what they are.

I have one that is my favorite as far as everyday work is concerned. The altar built for Circle is different, but this place is located on the mantle over the fireplace. I have a big round mirror over it, and on it are many objects both magical and beautiful. The Venus de Milo graces this space, as does my pentacle, cords, candles, crystals, stones, plants, athame, wand and censor. When a plant does get ill in the house, this is the place where it spends a complete Moon cycle. It usually does not even need this long. The space is highly charged. I can feel intense power emanating from the things that reside on this altar. I have done much work from this altar and its residual power remains. This power blends with the natural power of the witch and her surroundings.

I feel myself drawn to this particular altar when my sources ebb, and it rejuvenates me. I cannot remember a time when it has failed to do so. My daughter even loves to touch the things that are on it. She is learning the Craft and I do not mind if she looks at or touches things like the athame (remember, it is dulled).

The curious thing about every Wiccan or Pagan I have ever known is that altars are never fixed in a particular way. They are ever-changing and this makes them more powerful because they have been fussed with. I move things around as I use things for my work. They never go back into exactly the same place. This is not gospel, of course. But witches make use of their magical places. The movement of the altar reflects the essence of the move-ment of the universe. It also reflects the levels of spiritual understanding. Our world is forever changing. The movement of Wicca is what connects us to the Goddess, and with this connection comes the power of the witch.

My herbal pantry is in the kitchen. On a day-to-day basis, my herbal magic or medicinal herbology is done here. For a Circle, I move the things I need to the area of the Circle. But generally, not a day goes by when I don't work from the pantry. I have glass jars by the dozens, full of the things that hold the Mother's power. There are herbs and spices, mixing dishes and a cauldron, censor and incense (often mixed myself), and all the things I need to make my work happen. A small pouch of salt rests on a nail in the corner of the cupboard, to protect and purify the space. I have yarrow twigs for strength and an empty bottle with cork for the elemental aspects of the pantry. I mix muscle rubs from here, and brew teas and base oils, I work spells and talk to my spirit guides while I work. And I maintain a notebook of all that I do. I feel good here; I feel powerful here. My spells are well-researched and strong to ensure proper uses of the different ingredients.

The herbs are charged before use by holding them in my hands, palms together. In an alpha state I merge with the herbal vibrations. This is necessary so that when your work is done, enough of yourself has gone into it that the spell is completely identified with you, the creator. I also use my herbs for the environment and atmosphere of my home. I burn different ones for different reasons and I use a variety when spelling for others.

I have packets of herbs around the house and bags for protection in different spots. But generally, my house looks like many other homes—I have laundry waiting for me, too! I cannot twitch my nose and have it done (although many times I would like to). I, too, must make meals for my family and put away the groceries. The regular routines of the day are interspersed with the Craft around me and in me. I cook with herbs that mean something. Often my kitchen smells of thyme, rosemary, coriander, etc. I am either burning these for a scent or cooking with them.

I incorporate what I eat and drink into the work I do in the Craft. Not all of it, of course, as I enjoy fast food just like many other people. But if I am drinking black tea, for example, and I know someone in financial trouble, I will visualize that person as I drink it and spell for their prosperity. Black or China tea has wonderful properties, and prosperity is one of them. If you are going to drink it anyway, give it a reason to use its power. Give it a focus and it will respond. And remember, never waste the lighting of a candle. Every time you give birth to a flame, pray to the Goddess for the good fortune or healing of someone you know. If the candle is to be used strictly for atmosphere, the wish will cause it to burn more brightly because you know that your work has connected it to the greater Light.

The variety of ways to make magic is only limited by your imagination. You should incorporate what you do day-to-day into magic for those in need. It will come back to you three-fold so you might just as well draw whatever positive, loving energy you can, right?

It seems an absurdity to suggest that some witches are Green witches and some are not. The very essence of witchcraft comes from the rhythms and tides of the earth and sky. The term "green" used to refer to witches who were herbalists, but now, any witch who feels a conscious responsibility for the environment is considered a Green witch, and in my opinion that includes just about all of us.

In the Craft today, not all Wiccans have the opportunity to work with the environmental elements in their daily existence, as those of the Craft of yesteryear. Many witches find solace and comfort in reading, ritualizing and keeping their records and journals. Many live in highrise apartments in cities where herbal witchery is more difficult. But others must have some physical manifestation of the pulses of life on this planet.

The Green witch is generally thought of as a practitioner who uses things like herbs, plants, and any earthgiven item. It was once believed that Green Craft was exclusive to herbal doctors, but this is not the case. We are witches who use herbs everyday and often an herbal witch is a scentist. I love to develop new pot-pourris, incenses, and remedies that are based on ingredients with magical properties.

Whatever manner you choose for honoring the Mother, don't let Her slip from you. Naturally, I mean this in both a physical and a spiritual sense. You may not have the opportunity to have plants or herb cupboards or even a place where you can take a walk. But it is essential that a witch maintain a steady and open communication with Her. This is not a rule, but most Wiccans get a sense of restlessness if they do not touch base with the Earth on a more frequent basis than just the Sabbats. We need a continual exchange between us, and if we do not have it, we tend to whither. We feel adrift and we must work all the harder to come back to Her comforts again.

For those who have, for whatever reason, a rough time keeping a link with the Mother, here are a few suggestions.

• Always have as many herbs and plants that your space allows. You do not have to fill the space entirely, but grow something in your windows. Some herbs are easy to grow (parsley, basil, etc.), and can be cut just before they are to be used. You do not have to harvest them in crop-manner. They continue to provide you with fresh flavor all the time. Don't forget that they have magical properties that can work for you, as well. Check the local library for books on planting "household" herbs.

• Houseplants are another source of power from the Mother. They don't have to be herbs and they all have fundamental magical potencies. Many are hard to find in a book of plant powers, but you can choose them for other reasons. Here is a good rule of thumb when buying plants. It is not true in a few cases but generally it works. If the leaf is dark green and with no or few light markings, it will grow in the darker parts of the house. For those with few windows, philodendrons, succulents of various kinds, and other dark plants are all good choices. If you have filtered or direct light, try arrowheads, ivy, spider plants, or marble climbers. If your plant appears sick, put it on your altar. Water all plants a little each day rather than drowning them one day a week. It does not take a lot of money to cultivate house plants. Ask friends for slips from theirs.

• To get started with a small altar, if you do not already have one, a candle, incense, a pentacle, salt and water are all you need. Whatever you use for your altar, be sure it feels right. Pretty statues of the Goddess in any aspect can look lovely on an altar, as well as pottery bowls for your work. If a thing does not work in that spot, put it away and try again some other time. Enjoy the spot. It is a place of power.

• You can attune yourself with the Mother by having stones and crystals around you. Everyone has space for a crystal garden, no matter how small. Each stone will emit a vibration of its own and you can customize the garden to your own needs. If your house feels vulnerable, use stones with protective properties. If concerned about finances, add a few for prosperity, etc. Be creative and use containers that are appealing to the place and the eye. Anything will do. I know one Craftswoman who has a tremendous collection of beautiful pieces and the vibrations from them can be felt entering her home. She cares for them and nurtures them and they respond to her. They shine with an inner energy and yours can, too.

• Finally, the easiest method of all is to fill yourself with the gifts from the Mother. As you sit to eat your meal, take each bite of vegetable or fruit and literally feel its vibration as you merge with it. Taste it fully. Feel its texture and imagine its color. Each vegetable or fruit has all four elements within it. Each carries the spiritual essences of the elemental realms. These items require water to grow. Each went through an exchange process with the atmosphere of the planet. All required the warmth and the light of the sun to grow and survive (except, perhaps, mushrooms), and they each needed the firm foundation of the Mother to give them life. So you see, when you put food in your mouth, it is not just for the taste. Think about what you eat and absorb the elements through it.

Whatever method helps you stay in touch with our lovely planet, keep at it. Don't lose sight of your desired goal. If the method begins to lose appeal, try something else. But as a Wiccan, you should continually maintain a link between yourself and Her. She will nourish you, but you must reach out and grasp what she gives.

Chapter Ten

A VISUAL AID

Many religions or systems of belief provide visual schemes upon which to focus attention when meditating. In doing so, we develop a deeper feeling for the flow of beliefs within that system. The Cabala is a fine example to which I refer. The diagram of the Tree of Life is used by occult practitioners all around the world. It is a visual representation which triggers the very foundation of that system when used properly. This provides students with feelings of centeredness.

Wicca is a richly symbolic religion, full of deep traditions and methodologies that have proven effective. I developed the following symbolism for students of Wicca who have some difficulty understanding the deep purposes of our religion. The visual help-mate which I put forth may also benefit veteran witches by bringing them closer to the essence of the Craft as well. This symbolism is a visual representation of the beliefs and striving of witches. It works in conjunction with any of the wonderful writings on the Craft that are available today and it will enhance Wicca for any student who absorbs it.

As you can see, the background for this system is the pentagram (or the five-pointed star), as shown in figure 1,

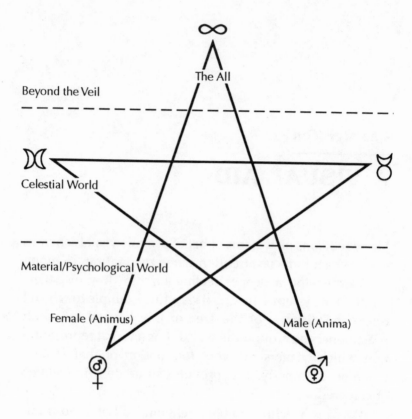

Figure 1. *A new perspective on the pentagram.*

above. The uppermost point stands alone; thus, the contemporary symbol of the white magic of Wicca. The reverse pentagram is used by some Wiccans as a representation of the material focus of the second degree,[1] however, many of us feel that until the connotation of satanic practice is lifted from it, we do not use the inverted pentagram, and have used other representations for our rituals.

---

[1]The second degree is the second level of knowledge in many wiccan traditions.

The star has been divided vertically to represent the female on the left side and the male on the right. The All at the top cannot be split because of its completely harmonic nature. By setting the pentagram out in this manner, we see that the God and the Goddess are gender representations of the All in the Celestial plane; the male and female are physical representations of the All in the material plane; the animus and anima of the female and male are representations of one aspect of the All in the mind of the individual. This is the harmonizing principle for our gender-specific species.

As we move down the horizontal divisions of the diagram, we see that the Goddess and God take their place between humans and the All. The work that we do, as human beings, takes its energy from the celestial world of the Goddess and God.

Blending with the material world is the psychological or emotional realm which houses the animus (male aspects) in women and the anima (female aspects) in men. These harmonic opposites exist in all of us but the awareness of their being is often hidden in the trappings of the social/physical world. Acknowledgment of them is necessary on the road to oneness with Mother Earth and Father Sky and All That Is. We need to know and care for the gender opposites that subtly effect our daily lives.

The pentagram is composed of one continuous line, which to Wiccans represents the cyclical nature of reincarnational existence. In this diagram, however, because the topmost point represents the All—and because we come from the All and must return to It after our education is done—there can only be two methods in the Way of the Witch. Both must be learned and then absorbed into the heart of the witch. This system enables the witch to be aware of both methods.

The first method shows a path on the diagram leading from the All in two directions—one to the female side and one to the male. This energy sparks a deep desire to capture the essence and meaning of the animus or anima within. It brings this essence back through the rational self to ensure a closer look at the Self (as a whole and harmonized individual, aware of the existence of both genders within), thus causing the male to travel forward to a clearer concept of the Goddess and the female to a clearer concept of the God. The achievement in recognition of the animus and the anima is necessary to bring into harmony the both-gender characteristic of the All. Once this understanding has been reached, much can be realized about personal hopes, fears, anxieties, insecurities, etc.

The second path to achieving harmony is the power coming from the Goddess and God directly to the gender-opposite human being. The Goddess sends Her force through the male and causes him to recognize the Goddess aspects and anima in him, thus imbibing him with Her power. The God sends force to the female, thus recognition of the male force within her enables her to harmonize. Both have a clear path to beyond the veil of the All.

As Wiccans, these visual paths help us see that we must deal with gender recognition on an emotional, material, celestial, and spiritual level as a total experience. If one or the other is lacking, the harmony is not attained. It is easier to recognize and relate to the Life Force as a singular gender rather than inspecting the other-gender side. To examine this side often requires that we lay bare any insecurities and beliefs we have held firmly for so long. This is difficult because an insecurity can provide something to associate with—be it good or bad.

In witchcraft, the recognition comes about in both ways discussed—because one eventually triggers the other to the practitioner. The first occurs when moving down figure 1 (on page 106) recognizing the no-gender status of the All, incorporating the Goddess and God into our lives as representations of the One (each with separate gender distinction) and finally reaching the material world where we ourselves hold one physical gender. The other brings recognition of the Celestial beings—Goddess and God, thus opening up our animus or anima and finally bringing us to our relationship with the All.

Chapter Eleven

A PROCESS OF INTERACTION

The very nature of Wicca and our belief in reincarnation causes practitioners to contemplate thought and behavior in accordance with, very simply, what reaction it will evoke. With the idea of negative and positive energy working in a cyclical manner, one can safely depend on the emissions of energy eventually returning to their source. The things that happen to us on a daily basis are the results of the kinds of energy we transmit into the world. With some kinds of negative behavior we can see an immediate response in our environment. Greater negative deeds may take longer, perhaps even lifetimes.

For example, you have run into a problem with a friend. If you react in a negative way (i.e., telling him or her off), you need look no further for your "reactionary" energy as you hammer your toe or trip and fall. You have immediate response in your environment for the negativity. The deeds themselves (the telling-off, the toe-stubbing, etc.) have really nothing whatever to do with what is really occurring. They are merely incidents that bring the energy into mundane representation. They are the byproduct of your actions and the return of the energy you emitted in the first place.

Perhaps some readers will find that this strikes them as a rationalization of each and every action in life. This is not so. If one truly accepts the possibility of reincarnation in a rational and logical way, then the responsibility for one's own actions and thoughts is a totally self-developing necessity. With each judgment of the self and its actions, the ability to make decisions (based in goodness) improves.

We must make decisions in our mundane lives but also between them. With the passing of each lifetime, we take stock of what has been learned and what yet needs to be learned. When we are proficient at pure action and thought, we move to another level of consciousness and education. We are no longer required to take on a physical form because we, through many lives, have gleaned all that we can from physical states of being.

As we ascend the ladder of "learning," we become more and more aware of the infinity of the cosmos and how truly vast it is. We become pure potentiality.

When our Selves have evolved to a state of pure joy and love, we merge with the All—back to where we started. We were parts of the whole, sent out to achieve what there is to achieve, both in the physical world and the worlds that exist beyond it. We must evolve to a state of being aware that we are the godstuff of the universes and that we will one day achieve that wholeness once more.

Wicca sees human existence as the way the Goddess feels her physical self. We are Her nerve endings on this plane. We touch for Her, we taste for Her, we love for Her, and we live for Her. Witchcraft pushes the practitioner to see this greater picture of what human beings have to deal

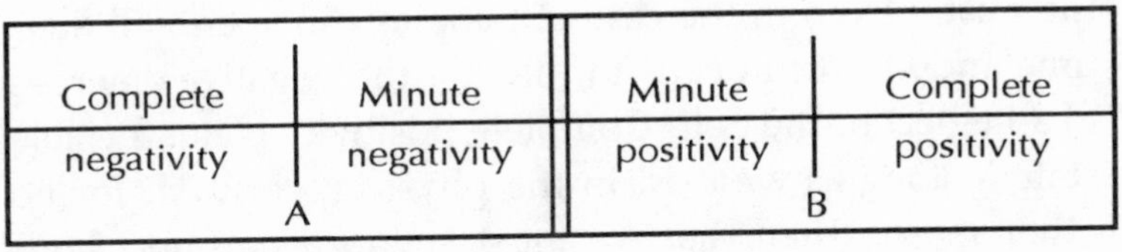

Complete negativity	Minute negativity	Minute positivity	Complete positivity
A		B	

Figure 2. *The scale of negative and positive energy.*

with. To be totally aware of one's own actions and language is to become closer to the Lady in whom we all reside as individual selves. Because the All is pure goodness, harmony, and light, we must strive to bring these aspects into our everyday lives. This awareness leaves little time for such self-defeating emotions as anger, jealousy, depression, or greed. These states are not only counterproductive, but they are the ones which cause us to do harm to ourselves and others.

When an emotion sits on the scale (see figure 2) at complete negativity, we know that this is self-defeating and destructive. But let us look also at the state of complete positivity. This state can be a causal force to throw us to the opposite end (complete negativity). If elation over something causes us to lose our self, then we have not maintained a healthy state. Perhaps in the state-between-lives, when we have no more need for the physical, we can move slowly toward the end that shows pure positivity. But with the burden of mundane existence—in the sense that we exist in a physical world—we must deal with emotions and actions that may cause us to resort to negativity.

Let us say, for example, that humanity in general stays within the area between *A* and *B*. We, through each incarnation, move toward the middle point—where harmony can emerge. But if we have moved outward along the scale in our thoughts and deeds, then harmony falls back into the mists. Even in the case of people who spend all their time and effort in deeds for others, the negative emerges in a neglect of the Self. Complete positivity is not a viable state as long as we exist in the physical world, if, for no other reason than that we must spend a portion of our time taking care of our physical needs. Jobs, children, loved ones, and homes all demand our time. We must keep ourselves relatively healthy in order to fulfill the jobs we set for ourselves. We must look at the things that happen to us as a teaching tool for our benefit. When we behave or speak in a manner that does no good whatever, then we must be prepared for disharmony in the reaction.

If we hold our position between A and B with steady movement toward the center, then we can maintain a strong semblance of harmony in our lives. This harmony allows us to be free from guilt, jealousy, and so on. Revenge is one negative emotion that takes up an incredible amount of time for some people. If allowed to blossom, revenge can move from just outside harmony to the far end of the negative side of the scale, often manifesting in brutality, harassment, murder, or suicide.

Consciousness must behave in a manner which compliments its "containmentary" forces. By this I mean the thing which contains the consciousness. Our consciousness in any given physical life is contained within the body and in turn within our environment. Our behavior (the manifestations of the consciousness) must express in accordance with that which contains the Self. We must act in a way that does not disrupt that container. We do not choose to walk into fire because we know that we will physically be burned. This is the complimentary behavior to which I refer.

If we are in a cyclical movement back to the All, the Greater Consciousness, then we must live in accordance

with that container as well. Pure potentiality and goodness cannot take up physical time or space, therefore, it
must exist in harmony with it. If we live and breathe and
have our very being within the body of the Goddess, then
we must behave as a cell does within our own bodies. Our
cells act in accordance with our needs. Just as stress is a
major cause for bodily disruption, so negativity in our
lives is a disruption of the Whole. We must seek to calm
the negative in our lives and only then will we be free to
create harmony and balance in the greater sense.

Because of this incredible need and desire for harmony, we strive to obtain it within the physical world. By
purchasing different items for recreation and entertainment, we only serve to clutter up what little space we have
in which the Self extends. The high-tech objects available
today have their own vibrations, as does everything in the
universe—animate and inanimate alike. But the difference
between the VCR and the computer used by a priest or
priestess of Wicca to keep notes and recipes is this: the
computer has been imbibed with the power of the witch's
work and the VCR has not. I do not decry the usefulness
of the VCR, but it does not hold the same strength of
energy. Therefore, it does not emit energy of a positive
kind into your environment nor does it give you something from which to draw.

It goes without saying that all magical and ritual
equipment is overflowing with energy that is there for the
taking. And of course, the most vital source of workable
energy comes from living things. Most people who are
pagan or anyone in tune with the cycles of the Mother
usually have animals and plants. I have two cats and
many house plants. I will plant in the spring what herbs
my space will allow. I draw a great deal from the things
around me. My cat knows when I am needing energy and

he is always quite free with it. Most pet lovers have a rapport with their animals that others do not understand. We know each other's moods and moments. It is through love that humans develop this relationship with their pets, and love is a very powerful magic, indeed.

Living things—be they plant or animal—not only emit energy for your use but in turn draw in energy. Things from the earth (plants, crystals, stones, dirt, etc.) have the purpose of drawing energy in and cleansing it. Similar would be the hemodialysis machine. It draws the blood from the patient and carries it through an artificial fibrous kidney and back to the patient. It releases the fluid which is harmful and drains it from the blood. So, too, do the things of the Mother. They draw in energy that is without vitality and recycle it. What is released after this process is the stuff of the Goddess—the vital, essential energy that we all require. I can literally feel the life energy when I am around my altar and the stones, herbs, and magical things. They are alive and they are strong.

This exchange of energy—that we do on a constant basis—is the motion of life. We exchange energy with other living things as a way of cleansing and purifying ourselves of the negative stuff of the mundane world. The existence of things and the exchange between, cleanses the energy. And because consciousness is energy, we are, in fact, cleansing our consciousness.

There have been many studies done involving the elderly and their interactions with pets or small children. Older people are able to draw from them the energy of life. This is a clear example of the power of joy. The every-day isolated existence of many elderly people means they have very little contact with other living things or beings. Because a drawing in of energy is the principle survival mechanism of life, these people lack any source. Give them a source and they draw eagerly.

If we cannot make an exchange of this vital life source, then we wither and die. Negative energy acts on us by accelerating the effects. If negative energy has no barrier (i.e., positive energy), then it can eventually become too much for us to cope with. Strong healthy energy provides us with a natural protection against the negative. And just as our skin protects our bodies, so the harmonic forces protect our consciousness. To continue an exchange of energy is our reason for being. We must maintain a state of interaction. Plants and pets will wither if left without love. Old people and sick people will, too. Mother Earth cannot survive unless we pour our love back into her. We draw from Her, therefore we must give in return.

Our exchanges with Mother Earth have declined with the advent of cement, steel, and numerous other distractions and barriers. We no longer walk to get from here to there. We cocoon ourselves within steel and plastic cars and never come in contact with Her. I do not presume to suggest that we give up cars or move back to a totally agricultural society. This is just not going to happen. But what I do suggest is to touch Her more often and to interact with Her more often. Touch and embrace not only the Mother, but people and animals and all living things. Reach out. You will be amazed at the response when you do. People find it hard to reach out for a touch or hug but if you make the first move it is not generally refused.

There is an old saying, "There but for the grace of God go I." This statement probably has a counterpart existing in all languages, religions, and cultures. For the Native North American, the sentiment is: "When you have walked a mile in your neighbor's moccasins." Each people of the world has a different way of expressing the idea of having to put yourself in the other person's place before you have any right to criticize.

Witchcraft also uses this tenet as a fundamental rule of thumb. Witches do absolutely nothing until we have examined this aspect. I call this process of examining Life to Life. With the advancement of the technical age, and the considerable time and money spent on pursuing the increase of personal entertainment systems and various escapist medias, human beings are now more than ever preoccupied with the self. The singular person. Our age, in one sense, is one of seeing to the needs of the "I, Me." This could account for the tremendous growth of the pagan religions in the past thirty years. We need to consider ourselves once more as part of a whole.

The way to love the self is to love outside the self. One does not come before or after the other. They are mutually dependent on each other—the self and others. I have never met truly happy or harmonious people who only love themselves. And I have never met people who truly love others without finding a deep sense of satisfaction and love in their own hearts. By the laws of polarity and balance, and by the very heart of logic itself, self-love and other-love must go hand in hand. They must, for they are opposites. They are as much a part of each other as are any other harmonious opposites.

The "principle of Polarity" which was advanced by M.R. Cohen, states "that members of such pairs are intelligible only in terms of contrast with each other."[1] Because we must know one to understand the other, we are left in a position of having to take the other guy seriously. By no means am I saying that you must put all else before your-

---

[1] M. R. Cohen, *A Dictionary of Philosophy* (London: Pan Books, The MacMillan Press, 1979), p. 279.

self, but I am saying that despite the fact that we are all human and have the failings that humans do, we must live as a unit rather than as separate entities. Those who believe in the theory of reincarnation have to see everything around them in the sense of being a member of the whole. We have chosen this life for the lessons it will offer and tolerance may very well be the key credit to pass the course.

A friend of mine, a priest of the Craft, was telling me about the change he sees in his tolerance and attitude toward people because of his years of witchcraft. He said that when he was 17 or 18, he saw the street person as someone who didn't want to work, or who didn't want a home, and so forth. The person was in that way because he allowed himself to be. If my friend could find a job, then so too could the person on the street.

But he told of the subtle realization that came about from life in the Craft. He said that now he understood that perhaps in this incarnation the street person chose (between lives) to learn very particular lessons and was in that process. With this came the awareness that my friend and the street person were part of the same Whole. Perhaps, in another lifetime, the positions would be reversed.

My friend now views living as a responsibility. He owns a restaurant and this past Yuletide he made many extra turkey dinners and took them down to our local mission. He feels that now he can take some responsibility for humankind because he belongs to the human race. He is a unit that is a part of the Whole, rather than an entity unto himself. As we move through the cycles of our lives, we understand that we will wear our neighbor's moccasins at some point, so perhaps we should take out insurance now by caring about what happens to our neighbor today.

As I said earlier, there has been a large return to paganism in recent years. *Pagan*, in older dictionaries, is defined as a person who leads a godless and unchristian life. Newer dictionaries define the term more positively. Pagans do not lead a godless life by any means! Our gods and goddesses are the key to our understanding of the Craft. However, most of us do lead an unchristian life because most Wiccans are not Christian, but then again neither was Jesus. We follow the moral axioms that were set forth by Jesus in the most fundamental way. Most Wiccans that I know follow the way of Jesus better than some Christians I know. The interpreters of the Bible and other holy documents, have confused and made complex the idea of achieving peace and joy in the world. Wiccans try to lead a life of tolerance and understanding but our ways and customs are not what a modern Christian might call "Christian."

Chapter Twelve

THE WITCH WITHIN

Wicca facilitates inner growth. Aside from the many things that a novice witch experiences, aside from the Lunar and Solar dances, apart from the herbs and stones of the Mother, and apart from the rich symbolism in ritual and spell, apart from all these things, the Witch must sort out his or her life's learnings. They must be rethought and recategorized. Students need to accept the lessons as they are experienced. We are here for a purpose and that purpose is to learn as much as possible and to find the Harmony of the Goddess. If that education requires that we throw out some preconceived thoughts and notions, then so be it. Just as my friend realized that the responsibility of those less fortunate is in the hands of everyone, including his own, so we all have lessons that make us rethink our past attitudes. All people will question "humanness" at some point. Witchcraft is a path of questioning. Not all information is available to everyone at once. We cannot just read it in a book or learn it by research alone. Much can be learned this way and should be, but we can only know if something is right for us after we have physically and emotionally absorbed a great deal of information.

For example, if we choose to start a hobby, we cannot go out and buy all the things we need without first purchasing an instruction book. We expend time and effort reading to get a full understanding of the project before we start it. If we don't do this we cannot be sure of just what we will end up with. And this is true of religions or beliefs as well. They have to be researched. The trick is that after we have done our study, we must allow ourselves some time for reflection.

When this reflection process begins, we realize that the concepts are making themselves known on a regular basis. Ethics have shifted and we no longer feel the same intensity of anger, jealousy, or bitter emotions. These feelings lessen because the knowledge we have acquired has caused us to question the very foundations of our lives.

A young lawyer I met years ago began his journey on the Wiccan path while maintaining his legal practice. He found himself starting to question everything, as this is the way of the witch. He questioned his work, finances, beliefs, and prejudices. He began to take on more cases of a humanitarian nature, and turned down those which he felt were environmentally or societally unethical. He refused cases of building foreclosures, evictions, divorce, etc. Rather, he began practicing law which would aid the underdog. He fought for tenant associations and the elderly.

He also started to take a good look at the companies in which he owned stock, and he sold those he found to be contributing to the loss of rain forest, or the cause of air pollution, or who sponsored massive cutbacks. He did not lose in the long run. He found himself in a better position because he relied on his own intuition and the power of the Goddess.

The nature of Wicca is such that we eventually realize the waste of time that negative emotions and behavior can create and we learn to understand the overall functioning of the human machine as a Whole. I don't think that a witch who is aware of the Mother, and Her gifts to us, could be comfortable contributing to the financial goals of a company whose works commit acts against the Mother. We deal with this problem on a daily basis whenever we need to purchase items that are not sold in ecologically sound containers. Hopefully we will be able to support manufacturers who are ecologically conscious.

The cyclical nature of the occult belief in many life-times, allows us to fix our own mistakes and the Witches Rede—and it harm none—allows us the freedom to avoid those mistakes. The Rede (see p. xii) is not easy to follow at first in absolutely every case. You must work hard to keep this motto at the forefront of your thoughts and to use it continually. Eventually it will become habit, but to begin with, it takes concentration and effort on the part of the new witch. If you use the Rede, the need for defensiveness is unnecessary. Why get defensive about something which you have thought about thoroughly? The need to do so is gone and this leaves time for other more enjoyable pursuits. If your actions have not or will not hurt anyone, including yourself, you need not defend them.

Sensory Perception

The term extrasensory perception has always baffled me. If we experience the standard five senses, these are known as sensory experiences. But if we are experiencing another sense which may not be common to all people, this is considered an extrasensory experience or ESP. We only use one tenth of our brain and we haven't a clue as to what capabilities the other portion possesses. If there are many more senses to be learned, then the people experiencing them are experiencing six, seven, or eight senses. These are not something outside the realm of sensory experience but, rather, something that a small percentage of human beings possess. Some people are born without sight. If sight is restored by surgery, this is not considered an "extra" sense. If people develop, through work, the ability to sense what is around on a different level, this, too, is not extrasensory. It is very natural. All humans have ability beyond the standard five senses, but many choose to ignore them or leave them dormant.

People who have unusual sense experiences are not crazy, or freaky, or anything else. For example, I conduct a very normal life; I am responsible for a family and my work. I have a good education and as far as I know, mental illness is not a difficulty my family has had to cope with. I, however, do not deny the existence of all my senses. They all work and they don't let me down. I cannot always describe what happens to me, because I am limited by a fixed vocabulary of reality. The success rates of my readings speak for themselves. I always tell my clients not to reveal anything to me during the reading. If they wish to discuss a situation and ask questions, this is done after the reading. My clients are happy and they return. I am able to tell them things I could not possibly know; the initials of a parent, a childhood nickname, the scent someone wore, or the location of lost documents. This is awareness. There is nothing distinctive in these abilities, I just choose to exercise the gifts given to me.

If you want to develop these other senses, you must be prepared for hard work and many possible disappointments. You cannot start piano lessons and play Mozart to perfection as a beginner. You must practice and visualize yourself succeeding. You must become aware of all that happens around you. If you have asked that a certain solution to a problem is the correct one, perhaps you will see a feather float down, or a squirrel cross your path, or you see a shooting star. Look for these things and be confident in your interpretations. Only you can decide how you want to reflect on a thing. As *The Charge of the Goddess* tells us—you must look within, for you will not find it without.

With the acquisition and fine-tuning of the other senses, responsibility is, without a doubt, deepened. If, when you do a reading for another person, you sense a very deep personal problem from the client, you cannot blurt out an offer of help. You must become sensitized to the feelings of others. "And it harm none," remember? In all that we do, this is the motto. Keep what you see to yourself if it will embarrass or hurt another. If you can find an opportunity in the cards to introduce the subject, then it is your moral responsibility to consider this and decide if saying something would be right. Then you may offer aid if possible. This will, at least, let the person know you care. He or she may never accept, but that person will know you are there.

In the field of moral and ethical philosophy, Immanuel Kant, a German philosopher of the 18th century, contributed his work entitled *Critique of Pure Reason*. His works are well worth reading, but there is one formula to which I wish to bring your attention. This is the Kantian Categorical Imperative; "Act only on that maxim which you can at the same time will to become universal law."[1] That is to say, behave in a way that you would wish could become a universal law, adhered to by everyone. Kant's Categorical Imperative is the Wiccan Rede. They are teaching the same ethical lesson.

Develop the gifts that are your birthright, use them wisely, and they will serve you faithfully the rest of your days. I often have a small ritual to thank the Goddess for giving these to me and for my love-filled life. This is the only work done in this ritual. Many times, instead of a token for the altar, I will pledge myself to the Goddess. I will determine a time for meditation and inward journeys. I will spend some time in pursuit of the deeper lessons of the Lady. I am thankful for all that She has been to me.

Growing Within

If you ask witches if they were drawn to the Old Religion as children, a vast majority will say yes. We have had a yearning, and have sought out that which has been with us since we can remember. Being a witch in an earlier life also causes people to find the Craft again. I can remember as a small child being fascinated by anything representing

---

[1]Will Durant, *The Story of Philosophy, The Lives and Opinions of the Greater Philosophers* (New York: Washington Square Press, 1961), p. 276.

the four elements. Fireplaces, wind in my hair, water, plants, and earth have always been things I love.

Richard Bach wrote many wonderful books that have an esoteric theme.[2] They center on the time/space question, the idea of parallel existences and theories of personal reality shifts.

People must pass through many stages on the road. Some stages are easier to handle than others, and there will always be more questions to answer. Over time, Wiccans feel the tug at the sleeve and must answer the call. We gain knowledge through books and if we are lucky, we connect with others in the Craft. We may, at first, feel silly doing ritual or spell work, but as time passes, we enrich our lives with the absolute certainty that the work is worth a great deal. No doctor would dismiss prayer as a healing agent. No matter how much of an atheist, a doctor would never tell a family that prayer will do no good. In Wiccan healing rituals, we center and send, just as with any form of prayer. We focus on the person who is ill, and we will that the power be sent to heal the illness.

Most witches wear white when a loved one has died. We feel that the person is continuing on a journey to knowledge. Yes, we are sad, but everyone must grow old and die. It's natural. All of us must pass the same fork in the road. We celebrate the privilege of having known the person dear to us, and we rejoice in the memories we have. These memories are ours to keep.

---

[2]If you would like to explore some of Richard Bach's books you may be interested in *Illusions: The Adventures of a Reluctant Messiah* (New York: Dell, 1981); *Jonathan Livingston Seagull* (New York: Macmillan, 1970); *One* (New York: Dell, 1989).

Because of our inner growth, we allow ourselves to view life-death-rebirth as a cyclical adventure. With this idea firmly embedded in our minds, we can see events — happy or sad — as experiences by which to grow.

Witches who are truly sure of their power — and of the power of love and joy — will walk the path and not worry about people who do not wish to accept our form of prayer. The path of witchcraft is a rich and positive journey of love, trust, and harmony. But remember, love, trust and harmony must start within each of us, and from there, the harmony will reach all over the earth.

Walking the Path

There are really no words to express the joy and peace of Wicca. We are practitioners of a religion far older than any of the organized faiths better known today. The Goddess has been a focus of celebration and life for tens of thousands of years. We recognize the joy of living and the cycles of our lives through the mysteries of She who gave us life. We take pleasure in the Sabbats of the Wheel, and we work very hard for those who need us at the Esbats of the Lunar pulse. We try to love for the sake of loving, and when we can be of help, we do our best. We, as women and men of the Craft must be patient, for the day will come when our beliefs are recognized as kind, loving and healing truths.

We walk the path seeking knowledge through the light and love of the Lady. It fills me with joy to know that many other Wiccans are working, together and alone toward a more peaceful world — a world of harmony, where children are loved, life is precious, and joy is the order of the day.

If you are a witch who works alone, either by choice or by necessity, remember that there are many brothers and sisters out there who really care for you and what your work contributes to our common goals. The Mother is within all of us, therefore we are intimately connected. Reach out and you will feel us beside you. Witches are reflections of the love of the Goddess and with Her help, we will span the distances of time and space to meet once more in Her arms.

Blessed Be!

The Great Design

The Plan, the Great Design,
the lives all woven,
all return, and then
return again.

The path is steep,
the way is tread alone.
But not alone, for She
embraces all.

The Self retires
to some far fantasy.
To live and love the One,
the quest is near.

The dawn
soft bands of dew and strips of gold.
The Crone departs,
the Maiden takes Her place.

The Mother's breasts
to nourish all who ask.
She omits none,
who seek the truth.

The power builds,
the cone maintains the source.
In readiness,
the dancers strike their pose.

The Source awaits,
and soon will set to task.
The power hums,
and time returns.

The chanters chant,
the Priestess raises high
the Cup of Life.
Her children know the place to which all pass.

                                                                            −J.S.T.

Appendix

The Sabbats

The Wheel of the Witches' celebrations can be conveyed in many different ways. The Farrars have supplied us with lovely mythical rituals that are unique and inspiring. Paddy Slade, in her book *Encyclopedia of White Magic*,[1] has set the sabbats out for us in a delightful country way, with journeys inward for each. Robin Skelton, in his work, *The Practice of Witchcraft*[2] has simplified the movements and has shared with us his own unique style. Many occult writers have contributed to the numerous styles in which to celebrate the witch's most important days.

The descriptions that follow are simple and condensed. The components described are the ones I find necessary in my celebrations of our Sabbats. The rituals you use are up to you as practitioners. These descriptions are compact information packages that will help the new witch complete the Sabbat preparations.

---

[1]Paddy Slade, *Encyclopedia of White Magic* (New York: Bantam Doubleday Dell, 1990; London: Hamlyn Publishing Group, 1990).
[2]Robin Skelton, *The Practice of Witchcraft* (Victoria, BC, Canada: Porcepic Books, 1990).

Samhain—October 31st

I start with Samhain because this is the Witches' New Year. Its historical origin is the feast of the dead in Celtic lands. It has developed into a time of considering the dead and of celebrating their return for a brief time. I generally leave candles lit in the windows to light their way, and we always have a jack-o-lantern at the door. Many contemporary aspects of the childrens' Halloween are pagan in origin, and in our home, because my daughter is young, we celebrate with both Halloween and Samhain.

For Samhain, I use fall colors in my altar decorations, and often have lovely colored leaves about the Circle. Reds, golds, oranges, and browns are all fall colors and they can be incorporated to make a fine looking feast table as well. Fall vegetables are at their best and should be plentiful at the feast of Samhain, as well as the supper of the following day.

The scent for this celebration is primarily apple, but I use cinnamon, rosemary, and pine tar. I also leave my circle rather dark for this Sabbat, as I find that the mysteries of the festival are more clearly understood. This is indeed the "spookiest" of the Wheel and it is perfectly all right to use this dark mystery in your festivities.

Yule—December 21st and 22nd

Yule and Christmas are celebrated hand in hand in many Wiccan households and the traditions for the two are very similar, mainly because the pagan aspects were borrowed from the Yule Sabbat for the Christian Christmas. This Sabbat helps to usher in the dark inner-working days of the winter months.

The colors I incorporate for this season are white, silver, gold, red, and blue. The Winter Solstice is a time for bringing in light and joy to a long cold winter. I burn holly leaves (saved from my plant the year before), pine, nutmeg, and clove.

Imolg—February 2nd

The feast of Imolg is the celebration of the first stirrings of spring in the womb of the Goddess. This is a time when bud and root are just finished forming and the bud is ready to make the journey out to reach the warming sun of spring.

Colors used for Imolg are generally confined to the darker hues. I find that as this holiday is a time for inward working, I feel most comfortable in black.

I use mint, cinnamon, fennel and coriander for the Imolg Sabbat, and if working in a group, we make use of this time to work in gender based groups. By this I mean that this is the only time of the Wheel when we split into groups of women and groups of men. We do inward work, but often the women will do work toward the easy birth for a friend or member, or the safe journey of a friend through the difficulty of feminine surgery. The men will often work toward the success of a childless couple to conceive, or the success of a friend in his job search, etc.

This is not confusing the laws of polarity, but rather, because the male and female vibratory rates are different, often at this Sabbat the genders can build a cone to directly relate to a gender-specific need.[3]

---

[3]The "cone of power" is a power peak raised in a circle by the energy gathered there. This energy is then released to energize the wishes of its creators.

The Spring Equinox—March 21st

This is a time to ring in spring. The nights and days are equal in length and the animals have left their cozy winter nests. The world is waking up and witches emerge after a long winter of quiet work.

The colors for this Sabbat are pale yellows, pale greens, and violet. I burn hyssop and witch hazel with just a touch of anise for my incense. Hyssop and witch hazel were used as an old folk remedy to ease some of the problems that animals have in conception and birthing.

This is a time to open ourselves to the sun and light of warmth, and to revel in the security of knowing spring is come.

Beltane—April 30th

Beltane is the festival of the hunt. The maiden rides to snare the king stag and to hopefully conceive a child of the Goddess. This is the Sabbat at which Arthur was to have mated with his sister Morgan La Fey.

At Beltane we use all the scents of spring and we decorate our altar with the first greenery of the season. We set the fire in the cauldron, and see it as our blessing to the Goddess for providing us with this rebirth.

Summer Solstice— June 21st and 22nd

Midsummer is a time of work and leisure. The nights are short and we are able to enjoy the summer days. The Faeries are about at this time and we leave a little something for them in the evening. This is a time for children and childlike play, a time to absorb the sun's warming rays and a time to sleep in the cool of the night.

I burn orange, lilac, mint, and fresh wild grasses. The altar is adorned with fresh flowers and we feast on the freshest that this season has to offer.

Lughnasadh—July 31st

This sabbat is in honor of the God of the Sky, the Sun, which is at its peak. This is a celebration of flowers, first harvests, and all that is in bloom around us. The colors I use are yellow, green, and blue.

I burn thyme, basil, and dill. And at Lughnasadh, I enjoy the planning of the feast around the fresh cakes and breads of the season.

Autumn Equinox— September 21st

The autumn equinox is a time for thanksgiving for the bounties of the harvest. We concentrate on the grain theme for decoration of the altar. The scents used at this time are savory, chives, and burdock. Our feasts contain harvest vegetables and there is plenty of popcorn for all. The colors used at the equinox are usually harvest colors. Deep gold, orange, and deep reds are favorites.

The Sabbats are key grounding times for a witch and we take them most seriously as a way of recognizing the gifts of the Goddess and of our work over the course of a year.

A note regarding the Spring Equinox, the Summer Solstice, the Autumn Equinox and the Winter Solstice is necessary here. These times of the year occur when the psychic veils are at their thinnest. The bonds which hold us to our level of existence can become stretched, and if caution is not taken, an inexperienced witch may find himself or herself in a position of fright or confusion. Before beginning any psychic development at these times, consult with an experienced witch if possible. If it is not possible, then go about your work slowly and with conviction in your heart. Let the lessons come at their own pace and don't try to rush into anything.

BIBLIOGRAPHY

Bach, Richard, *Illusions: The Adventures of a Reluctant Messiah*. New York: Dell, 1981.

_____. *Jonathan Livingston Seagull*. New York: Macmillan, 1970.

_____. *One*. New York: Dell, 1989.

Bradley, Marion Zimmer, *The Mists of Avalon*. New York: Ballantine Books, 1985.

Cabot, Laurie, *Power of the Witch*. New York: Delta, 1989.

Cohen, M. R., *A Dictionary of Philosophy*. London: Pan Books, The MacMillan Press, 1979.

Conway, D.J., *Celtic Magic*. St. Paul, MN: Llewellyn, 1990.

Crowther, Patricia, *Lid off the Cauldron*. York Beach, ME: Samuel Weiser, 1981.

Durant, Will, *The Story of Philosophy, The Lives and Opinions of the Greater Philosophers*. New York: Washington Square Press, 1961.

Encyclopedia of Witchcraft and Demonology. London: Octopus, 1974.

Farrar, Stewart, *What Witches Do*. Custer, WA: Phoenix, 1983; London: Sphere, 1971.

Farrar, Janet and Stewart, *A Witches Bible, Volumes 1 & 2*. New York: Magickal Childe, 1981. Now available from the same publisher under the title, *A Witches Bible Compleat*.

Holzer, Hans, *The Truth about Witchcraft*. Richmond Hill, Ontario: Simon and Schuster of Canada, 1969.

Medici, Marina, *Good Magic*. New York: Prentice Hall, 1988.

Ryall, Rhiannon, *West Country Wicca, A Journal of the Old Religion*. Custer, WA: Phoenix, 1989.

Skelton Robin. *The Practice of Witchcraft*. Victoria, BC, Canada: Porcepic Books, 1990.

Slade, Paddy. *Encyclopedia of White Magic*. New York: Bantam Doubleday Dell, 1990; London: Hamlyn Publishing Group, 1990.

Strieber, Whitley, *Cat Magic*. London: Grafton Books, 1987.

Valiente, Doreen, *Witchcraft for Tomorrow*. Custer, WA: Phoenix, 1978.

Weed, Susan, *Healing Wise*. Woodstock, NY: Ashtree, 1989.

A practicing witch since childhood, Janet Thompson has been a Wiccan High Priestess for twelve years. She holds a B.A. in classical and medieval folklore with a minor in philosophy from the University of Windsor. She is a certified Master Herbalist consultant, lives in Canada, and enjoys writing both fiction and non-fiction.